2

GAZELLE-BOY

JEAN-CLAUDE ARMEN

GAZELLE-BOY

ILLUSTRATED BY THE AUTHOR

Translated from the French by

Stephen Hardman

UNIVERSE BOOKS

NEW YORK

ORIGINAL TITLE

L'Enfant Sauvage du Grand Désert
(Delachaux & Niestlé, Neuchâtel)

Published in the United States of America in 1974
by Universe Books
381 Park Avenue South
New York, N.Y. 10016

© Delachaux et Niestlé S.A., Neuchâtel
(Switzerland), 1971
English translation © The Bodley Head Ltd 1974

Library of Congress Catalog Card Number: 73-82104

ISBN 0-87663-174-X

CONTENTS

'To all of us there comes that towards
which we incline more or less obscurely.'
Spinoza, *Ethics* (from the *clinamen* of Lucretius)

'Every Element of this world is a Question,
an impossible whole with a thousand faces
like the Dodecahedron of Plato.' Shri Aurobindo,
Heraclitus and Hindu Thought

Rio de Oro (Spanish Sahara): Land of the gazelle-boy.

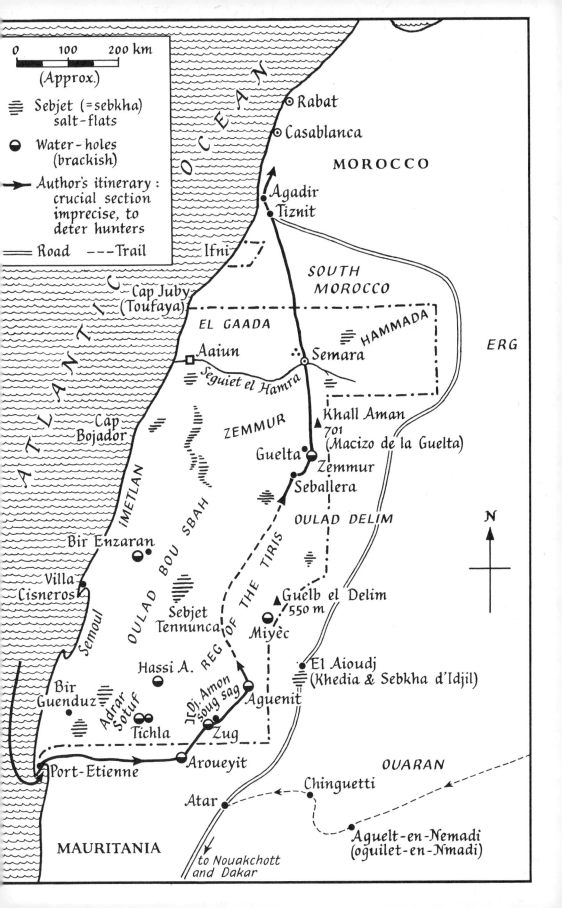

Scale: 0 — 100 — 200 km (Approx.)

Legend:
- ☰ Sebjet (=sebkha) salt-flats
- ◖ Water-holes (brackish)
- → Author's itinerary: crucial section imprecise, to deter hunters
- ═ Road --- Trail

ATLANTIC OCEAN

MOROCCO

⊙ Rabat
⊙ Casablanca

● Agadir
Tiznit

Ifni

SOUTH MOROCCO

HAMMADA

ERG

Cap Juby (Toufaya)

EL GAADA

☰ Semara

□ Aaiun

Seguiet el Hamra

Cap Bojador

ZEMMUR

▲ Khall Aman 701 (Macizo de la Guelta)

Guelta ●
◖ Zemmur
● Seballera

IMETLAN

OULAD BOU SBAH

OULAD DELIM

N

Bir Enzaran ◖ ●

Villa Cisneros ●

Semoul

☰
REG OF THE TIRIS

▲ Guelb el Delim 550 m

Sebjet Tennunca

◖ Miyèc

Hassi A. ◖

● El Aioudj (Khedia & Sebkha d'Idjil) ☰

Bir Guenduz ● ☰

Adrar Sotuf ◖◖

J. Dj. Amon soug sag ◖

Aguenit ◖

Tichla

Zug ◖

☰

Aroueyit ◖

Port-Etienne

OUARAN

● Chinguetti

Atar ●

MAURITANIA

to Nouakchott and Dakar

● Aguelt-en-Nemadi (oguilet-en-Nmadi)

AUTHOR'S FOREWORD

'The approach to the problem is more important than
the problem itself . . . for your prejudices, your fears
and your hopes will colour it. The correct relation results
from a lucid approach without selection.' KRISHNAMURTI

This is the record of an actual experience.

Wild children who have been adopted by animals, and who have grown up among them, are not always myths. And the reality is often much more extraordinary than fiction or an embellished account of the facts.

The celebrated novelist, Rudyard Kipling, contributed in no small degree to the spreading of confusion in the minds of the large public which was nurtured in childhood on his beautiful story of Mowgli. Although he started from fact, the author allowed himself to be carried away by his imagination, transforming the reality and sowing doubt in the minds of scholars, researchers and the curious.

Walt Disney, going one better than the 'father' of the wolf-child of India, made an even more fanciful film of the story, just at a time when the question was at last beginning to assume its true dimensions among men of science, in the light of recent studies on Behaviour and Environment.

Moreover, the inward attitude of approach to the event – the subject of this book – proved to be of unforeseeable importance. If it is purely conceptual, we merely continue the sterile method which proceeds from the known to the known and reduces the unknown to the known.

It is therefore important to prepare oneself inwardly for such an extraordinary encounter.

PART ONE

1. PRELIMINARIES

At the time of the astounding discovery related here, I knew nothing about wild children. Abruptly confronted with the reality, I had to set about studying the problem on my return from the Great Sahara Desert.

It seems that fifty or so of these creatures have been discovered since the year 1344, among them the famous wolf-children found in India by the Reverend Singh and the no less famous discovery related by Professor Itard in his report on the *Sauvage de l'Aveyron*, which has been the subject of a recent film. Obviously, the figure mentioned above does not include wild children who have not had the 'good fortune' to be brought to the attention of persons of authority and competence.

Previously, like anyone else, my notions had been limited to the myth of Romulus and Remus and Rudyard Kipling's embroidered narrative in *The Jungle Books* – in short, nothing really credible.

On the other hand, to the best of my knowledge none of these singularly-fated children was studied at liberty in his natural milieu, not even the child found by Professor Itard; similarly, again to the best of my knowledge, no photographs were ever taken of a wild child living among the animals which had adopted and reared him.

The extraordinary experience recounted in this book is the most moving to have befallen me in the course of five years of travelling round the earth and staying in 'forbidden' regions or in little-known parts of the world which have been explored only in a haphazard manner.

2. APPROACH

After a solitary crossing by camel of the Majâbat-al-Koubrâ – the 'Djouf' of the old maps and the largest forgotten desert in the Sahara, an utterly barren expanse worthy of the vast and partly unexplored Rub'al-Khâli, a desolate region of southern Arabia – I set off once again into the desert, with the intention of tackling a territory at that time difficult of access to foreigners: the Rio de Oro or Spanish Sahara.

Being French and not Spanish, I resolved to penetrate secretly, silently and discreetly into this region of the Great Desert, with a view to crossing the most remote and least travelled part of this strange land, the *Reg* of the Tiris.

* * *

A single pack-camel and a store of simple 'rations', determined by fairly long experience and native practice: dates for the driver, spare fodder for the vehicle.

A tunic and a Moorish *djellaba* (for coolness). A small block of magnesian salt for protection against thirst and fatigue, the secret recipe of the ancient caravans. A hundred litres of water in Moorish skins reinforced like Norwegian 'hay-boxes' against heating and evaporation (permanganate added to prevent the water from deteriorating). A supplementary luxury liquid, readily available for self-service: the milk of my female desert ship, to make the bitter green tea more palatable.

As on my journey into the other forgotten desert, I shall not be following tracks, but simply heading in a straight line (or as straight as possible). Rather than use a compass, I shall, like the nomads, follow the regular orientation of the dunes, aligned in the direction of the prevailing wind; and for the approaches to a water-hole, I shall follow the converging trails of wild animals.

Thus equipped, I cross a frontier indistinguishable in this immensity and advance, stage by stage, towards the heart of the little-known Tiris, allowing the hottest part of the day and the depth of the night to pass me by as I sleep in bivouac.

* * *

One evening, the far south begins to flash with heat-lightning. A sudden awakening in the middle of the night: panic-stricken animals running in all directions, a tidal wave of black water rushing along the bed of a dried-up *oued* and stretching out beneath a moon encircled with a sinister halo.

From the bank I watch a shoal become an island on which an incongruous medley of animals huddle together; species ordinarily hostile to one another seem to refuse combat. An impromptu paradise born of misfortune.

* * *

The next stage brings me to a nomad tent, where I am offered the ritual three glasses of mint-tea. The salutations are never-ending; a Moor of the nomad tribe of the R'Gueïbat Lgouacem, slender, lithe, draped in his flowing night-blue *deraâ*, his black hair dishevelled, stares deep into my eyes: a forehead of dry sun and cold stars, eyelids lined with antimony (that secret protector against sand-storms and reflected suns). The aroma of the green tea swirls in the bitter musk of the wind.

A *tidinît* (a small lute) and then an *ardîn* with twenty-two strings give out their airy music under the nimble fingers of women wearing amber neck-laces. The rings of voluptuous scarlet cornelian which they wear on their toes gleam through their sandals of oryx-skin. As the first stars appear, one of the women stands up, shrouded in veils, tall, hieratic, and begins to sing, dance and mime the traditional improvised *izlan*, a quatrain in honour of the guest:

'He has come:
the bullet has not ravished him.

19

He is strong as the sun:
the sand does not burn him,
the stone does not pierce him.'

* * *

I set off again on my camel, which shifts and spits as the flies swarm round.

The noonday hours pass in immobility. The little Moors of the clan, quite naked, and then their elders, like ephebes with gazelle's eyes, amuse themselves with fireside games, trying to make columns of hot sand rise as high as possible, or playing with hypnotised horned vipers, turning them rigid as a dead stick by laying them gently on their backs, then making them jump like springs with a smart blow from a real stick.

A frail little tame gazelle of the Dorcas species, with the large eyes of a houri, has a rough time with the children of the caravan as it is shoved, pushed from behind and knocked head over heels; they do the same with a poor shabby-looking she-goat, not to mention more dubious and distinctly Freudian games. Goat and gazelle sniff at each other's muzzles with an air of sad connivance.

* * *

Now, unfolding before me, is the vast salt plain of Tikla, a double shimmering sky. Ridges of old red sandstone proclaim the Djebel Amon-Soug-Sag, leading to gorges of fissured sandstone at the 'pass' of Meksem-Soug.

Leaving my wind-footed friends, I head due north, straight for the Tiris, which lies not far away. Between red and black blocks of magnetite iron, some little wild Dorcas gazelles swerve in and out, living dreams drawn from a glimmer of light. My tame fennec – a desert fox – seems to want to chase them, leaping about like a puppy.

* * *

The Tiris begins to unfold in an immense *reg* or *râg*, a plain of marl, gravel

21

The nomad improviser and the master of the caravan.

and splintered pebbles stretching as far as the horizon. From time to time, high tabular towers of old red sandstone rise up like look-out posts on this strange glimmering ocean, blackish or rust-coloured. In places, this impossible soil exudes what looks like burst blisters, and then becomes *heïcha*, a curious scaly gypsum pitted with holes and caves filled with water; a thousand reflected suns seem to dance between the high organ-pipes of the look-out towers.

In the evening everything bursts into flame below purple and violet cirrus clouds; the illuminated stone towers resound with a jarring of uncanny muffled echoes.

Prehistory at ground-level: hundreds of axe-heads of pink sandstone, arrow-tips of quartzite and sea-green phthanite. Prehistory in signals against the sky: curious twin menhirs, V-shaped monoliths, spring up between the high stone towers.

Strange reefs, like steep-sided islands, dance in mirages on a horizon palpitating under the heat; the mirages are turned topsy-turvy beneath the anvil of the torrid sun at its zenith. Skating rocks seem to come to life on their slides of smooth clay, describing a mysterious geometry.

Out of human weakness I try briefly to beguile the intensity of the heat with my own personal cuisine: *varan* (a carnivorous desert saurian) grilled with rice and the white truffles of the desert, then covered in fresh cream from the camel's milk and garnished with a few plump grasshoppers, black and corseted with red stripes – the whole flavoured with the droppings of fennec, camel and gazelle. Special menu for the fennec: snails in milk – popular fare for my beast of burden: an extra ration of *hâd*, thorns included.

* * *

In the hollow of a crescent-shaped dune (how it came to be in the middle of this infernal plain I cannot imagine) I unexpectedly come across some nomads who are not like the others – Nemadis, it would appear, a cross-breed of gipsy and Moor. Their simple camp for the night consists of gazelle-skins on a framework of stray roots. Cakes of salt lie in plaited straw beside baskets of dried Uromastix lizards. A solitary and seedy-looking old camel carries everything.

Wild games as the caravan halts.

The first dazzling vision, against the fiery face of the rising sun.

24

How curious to find these people so far advanced into the heart of the desert: could they be on some frantic hunt, or pursuing a migration of antelopes? These Nemadis are just like those who welcomed me at the end of my journey into the vast forgotten desert of the the Majâbat-al-Koubrâ: the poorest people in the Great Desert, but also, in their proud detachment from all encumbrances, the happiest, most carefree and gracious, entirely dependent on hunting the antelope, which is brought to bay by a hound with a muzzle like a jackal and shot with the old flintlock rifle (in earlier days, with bow and arrow) – 'what does tomorrow matter?'

* * *

Under the stars and beside the first fires, after an unusual meal of browned crickets and lizards crushed in a neolithic grinder, a handsome ephebe, dressed in a short indigo-blue tunic in the Nemdaï manner, recites the fable of the Jackal and the Fennec, interspersed with melodies on the nomad flute.

Then, with a matter-of-fact air, he recites the unlikely story about a little Moor who is adopted by ostriches and can run as fast as they (!?), quenching his thirst with the juice of wild fruits.

In spite of my difficulty in understanding certain elliptical turns of phrase, the particular mode of expression, far removed from that of the Arabic fable, makes me think 'there is no smoke without fire . . .' The events of the story would appear to have taken place two or three generations ago.

Noticing my intrigued look, the young Nemdaï comes up to me and promises me a much greater surprise of the same kind, at a *marhala* (stage) of one day's march (*nazir-at-yoûm*).

The Nemdaï youth recounting and miming the fable
of the Jackal and the Fennec.

3. DISCOVERY

The star heralding the dawn pales in the half-light. The stone watch-towers turn to a reddish old-gold. The arc of a corona emerges and glistens on the purple and green cirrus clouds of the horizon, announcing the sun. At the first beam of the rising disk, the sands begin to hum and the *guelb* (stone towers) strike up their clamour, following the immutable ritual of the desert.

Suddenly, my young improvised guide, his excitement tinged with a strange fear, points a finger towards the immense purple disk. I see nothing in particular. I strain my eyes and still see nothing. What keen sight these nomads have!

At last, strangely as in a dream, I see advancing towards me an outline, thread-like and incandescent, a naked human form; it is slender and with long black hair, galloping in gigantic bounds among a long cavalcade of white gazelles.

What can it be? A child living with gazelles, like the other with his ostriches? A vision of some unknown, fabulous creature in a world apart, gone as suddenly as it came. In the life of everyone strange signs sometimes appear.

My young guide has also vanished. Obviously, he must have thought he had seen one of the 'jinn' or genies that are both feared and revered by all nomads of the desert.

* * *

Approaching what I presume to have been the place of the apparition, I soon discover traces of tiny and obviously human feet, sometimes several metres apart, the weight resting on the front part of the foot and hardly making any impression on the sand, revealing a rare suppleness, the human prints blending with the rhythm of the bounding prints of the gazelles.

After several hours' march, the prints lead me to the foot of a long *guelb*, reddish and glowing. In a fold in the wall is the mouth of a fissured gorge, like a passage leading to the end of the world. Here I find a tiny oasis, virgin and wild, covered with tangled masses of thorn-bushes and flowering tamarisks and crowned by a few rather threadbare date-palms.

From one of the bushes a slender white form springs, a gazelle which immediately begins to pull up ball-shaped roots of *dhanoun* – the desert's principal survival food. A large male, holding his horns high, comes forward in his turn. Some fawns prance about.

Suddenly, I see blue flashes against jet-black hair, as a child with a bronzed and slender body darts from the same bush, throws himself at the unearthed roots, teeth first, peels them with clicks of his tongue, then cuts them up frantically with his incisors.

A gazelle lifts its head and puckers its muzzle. Curiously, the child does the same with his nostrils – and then, in a twinkling, they all disappear into the depths of the gorge. I have been scented, I say to myself; this wretched wind has changed direction, setting itself against me.

4. MAKING CONTACT

Retiring for the night a few miles away, at the foot of another *guelb*, stretched on my saddle-cloth and my Addax antelope skins, in the Nemdaï fashion, I await the following dawn for a new 'assault'.

* * *

Returning to the intriguing little oasis, I see neither child nor gazelles.

I decide to follow a line of droppings, prints of toes and hoofs, which lead me to the huge porch of a rock-shelter.

An almost unbearable smell of stale ammonia and wool-grease betrays a long sojourn under the walls of the shelter. The flies are also intolerable. I find some gazelles, but engraved in the rock-face, with solar symbols between the horns, a sign of Tanit and pre-Islamic spirals of enchanting mystery.

* * *

I return again at dawn on the third day.

The real gazelles have come back. In an opening in the thorn-bushes the child himself appears at last in profile, his hair over his shoulders like a horse's mane.

He catches sight of me, his eyes staring in amazement, perhaps even terror, though I too am hidden behind an isolated cluster of thorn-bushes. The game of hide-and-seek begins again.

Not knowing what to do next and weary of waiting on this scorching grill, I suddenly have an idea. Remembering from my childhood the *galoubet*, a three-holed flute used in Béarn by trainers of Pyrenean bears, I begin to play, sitting in Arab fashion, a few simple repeated notes on a little Berber

A sentry-gazelle.

flute, a Moorish *raïta*, making use of the syncopated trills of the crickets around me (during long periods of solitude in the desert, this is a universal and by no means ridiculous way of passing the hours).

After several attempts, I see him again in the opening in the bush, at first appearing furtively, then for longer and longer. A curious, extremely mobile expression, with traces of a frightened stare.

* * *

On the following day I adopt the same stratagem; fear gives place to a semblance of astonishment. As the sun sinks, a little gazelle advances alone, curious, apparently confident like all young animals, then halts in the no-man's-land of observation. The child, as before, stares quizzically.

Fifth day. As I play my flute again, the fawn of the previous evening (it appears to be the same) advances and dares to sniff my toe, then licks it. The child watches from a distance, as if transfixed.

Next day. A female gazelle, barely at the age of puberty, comes towards me while the little one licks my hands.

It seems that this is some kind of code signifying acknowledgement, contact, and almost recognition; the idea becomes more and more clear in my mind. Why, 'in reply', should I not imitate these gestures? I believe I saw two gazelles behaving thus with each other on the previous day, behind the hedge of thorn-bushes. If in fact the child is totally 'wild', he is bound to 'understand' from his 'observation post' and thus enable me to accelerate my tactics of approach; if he has been 'educated' by his animals, everything must surely follow the same pattern.

So I decide to lick the first little animal – not with the heavy licking of a dog, but in its own discreet gazelle fashion, with rapid, delicate little movements of the tongue.

Immediately, my approach tactics seem to make progress. A few moments later, a large female gazelle, older than the other, comes three-quarters of the way towards me and jerks its head twice in the air; almost at once, the child comes out of his hiding-place, while the young gazelle continues to lick my hands.

32

Between two stone towers like organ-pipes. The habitat of the boy and his animals seen from the south-west, with the 'look-out' gazelle, and the strange lenticular clouds of the desert.

The child, now clearly visible, shows his lively, dark, almond-shaped eyes and a pleasant, open expression (not sullen like wolf-children and other children reared by carnivorous animals); he appears to be about ten years old; his ankles are disproportionately thick and obviously powerful, his muscles firm and shivering; a scar, where a piece of flesh must have been torn from the arm, and some deep gashes mingled with light scratches (thorn-bushes or marks of old struggles?) form a strange tattoo – not always a life of paradise!

* * *

The following day. A strange order, a sort of protocol, becomes apparent as the senior male of the herd finally grants me 'recognition' with the end of his black, wet nose, while the child, advancing a few steps nearer, starts to roll his shoulders like a Pyrenean bear.

Ninth day. As I continue to play from time to time on my Berber flute (but is this of any use now that a 'code' has been established?), the child draws imperceptibly nearer, halting and moving back, then coming forward again. I have to remain quite still, avoiding quick gestures or any inadvertent movements. (Those who shoot waterfowl also know this long and monotonous discipline.)

The senior male of the herd, an old giant with eroded horns, keeps me waiting for his 'accolade'. Then, only a short distance away, I take the initiative by miming the second 'signal', the little licks of the tongue. So much for the petty-bourgeois rules of human civility! Once, I recall, the Tibetans of the Ladakh greeted me in their traditional manner, sticking out their tongues! (A misinterpretation on my part, which would have been quite logical for a Westerner, would have dispatched me to the next world – just as dogs and cats are eternal enemies because their signals are diametrically opposite in meaning.)

My male gazelle (which I have every reason to believe is the leader of the whole herd, and possibly of the child also) then comes right up to my face (I was going to say my muzzle!) and finally licks it in the same manner, after exploring different parts of my person with his nose.

34

Immediately, everything seems to gather momentum in the child, who comes up to me and sniffs my toes, still showing a few furtive traces of fear, despite his great boldness, and fitfully screwing up his nose, after the manner of his adoptive mentors.

Then he gives me a few little licks, first on the legs, then on the fingers. With little cries from the back of his throat, probably marks of joy, this strange child of nature incapable of all human language seems to be trying to make himself understood.

Now we are face to face and it is my turn to resume the initiative. I move my 'civilised' nose slowly towards his; my partner does likewise, the two of us remaining there curiously, like two cats acknowledging each other.

My turn again. But fear checks me: how can one lick another human being, even furtively, without appearing ridiculous? But, once again, inhibition is quickly overcome, for I have been accustomed to using many different and sometimes improbable sign-languages among the human inhabitants of the earth.

I have just made up my mind when the boy suddenly darts his tongue at the tip of my nose. In a flash, without further reflection, I respond in the same manner. (I think this is how it happened, though my memory of this moment is no longer fresh, and in the travel notes which I made at the time I did not record every detail of incidents as they occurred.)

The long days of waiting, the cramp, the infernal sun, the vicious flies, the scorching ground, the weariness of this exhausting perseverance, all are now forgotten as I experience the transparency and plenitude of a new state, of a rare 'communication' (later, perhaps, I shall be obliged to devise a new strategy to make this same 'communication' credible to my two-footed brethren in Europe dressed in their ties and bowler hats) – but also a painful moment of extreme intensity in which I must hold my own, as in the thick of some mighty battle; an instant of deadlocked violence, as in all great passions, which confers meaning and value on an existence.

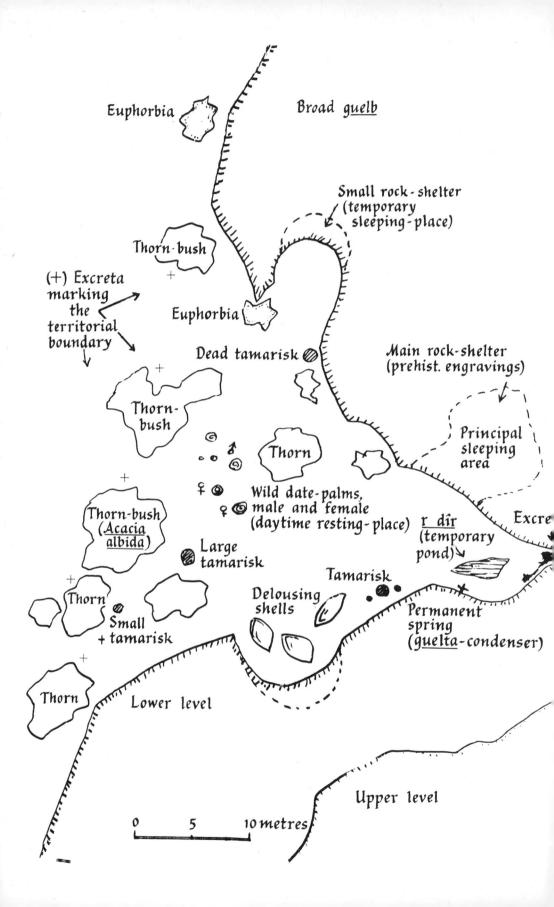

Euphorbia

Broad _guelb_

Small rock-shelter
(temporary
sleeping-place)

Thorn-bush

(+) Excreta
marking
the
territorial
boundary

Euphorbia

Dead tamarisk

Main rock-shelter
(prehist. engravings)

Thorn-
bush

Principal
sleeping
area

Thorn

Wild date-palms,
male and female
(daytime resting-place)

Thorn-bush
(_Acacia
albida_)

r dîr
(temporary
pond)

Excre

Large
tamarisk

Tamarisk

Thorn

Delousing
shells

Permanent
spring
(_guelta_-condenser)

Small
+ tamarisk

Thorn

Lower level

Upper level

0   5   10 metres

5. DAILY LIFE

The child, now quite without fear, like his animals, allows me to penetrate into the heart of his little oasis, illuminated with thorn-bushes bearing crimson flowers from which black xylocopa with iridescent wings fly out (these hymenoptera are commonly found in the desert). Catkins of tamarisk loose their pollen on the wind, like gold-dust, in a buzzing of emerald-hued coleoptera; fat hairy wasps and beetles cluster together on the oozing gum of acacias. The gazelles continue to sniff my legs, which become so entangled in muzzles that I am almost knocked head over heels.

My gazelle-boy makes for a seeping rock, sucks in the hesitant drops and then laps up those which fall, with a long pause between each drop as if to savour its taste.

Below, a little pool fringed with emerald-green swarms with tadpoles. High up, towards the top of the gorge, *sirlis* (a kind of desert lark) hover and swirl with their 'song that falls from the sky' (an expression used by Nemdaï hunters): *tiwit, pitiwit . . . tiwit, pitiwit . . .* a call as airy and diaphanous as the light foliage of the tamarisk, flitting to and fro above all the hummings of insects in an oasis born of a tiny spring, a primitive refuge overpopulated by contrast with the implacable silence of the desert.

* * *

With a few leaps the child heads for another corner of his oasis. I watch him sniffing almost incessantly, his neck stretched, his face to the wind, his nose continually jerking in little convulsive movements, his herd following behind him or leading him in turn.

He also sniffs the flanks of his animals, sprigs of brushwood, bits of thorn-bush, flowers, berries, fallen dates, balls of dung, traces of urine. Dare I add that his nose also finds its way to his animals' hindquarters (politely speaking)? – a particular feature of his 'education' which the supposedly 'civilised'

Principal habitat of the boy and his gazelles: the oasis-refuge.

human race will find difficult to understand; but the psychoanalysts say that roughly the same takes place, at an unconscious level, in homo sapiens, the creator of the highest spiritual values and of the thermonuclear bomb!

As regards this latter code of acknowledgement, I admit that I do not go so far as to reply in like manner, in spite of the anti-conformism which I have acquired as a traveller and explorer 'at home and abroad' who has witnessed far stranger sights.

* * *

The day after the decisive confrontation, I begin to play my music again. The child rolls his head and then his shoulders, as if he were being rocked; from time to time his hips start to sway. Then he resumes the same nose-to-nose gesture, like the ancient Maori kiss, exchanging a few little sniffs and licks with some twenty languorous-eyed gazelles.

Meanwhile, I notice the child's curious habit of twitching his ears and scalp at the slightest unusual or suspicious noise, his muscles tense and spasmodic – rather like the herd.

But I also become increasingly aware of the existence among all these animals of certain murmurs, eructations, little cries and, in particular, signs of the head or the hoofs which seem to have some common significance – perhaps even a new universe of 'codes' to decipher little by little.

The whole herd rolls about in curious clay depressions, the hair of child and gazelles mingling in clouds of grey dust. They use shells to rid themselves of parasites and the smectite clay for cleansing grease and sweat – the ideal solution to the Saharan traveller's eternal problem: how to clean himself without squandering precious water.

* * *

The boy climbs on all fours (left hand with right leg and vice versa, like the Polynesians) up one of the date-palms of his little paradise, bolting the few bitter green dates, both pulp and stone. At another moment, one of the male palms is stripped of some of its clusters of pollen, which form a strange sulphur-coloured haze.

39

Evolution according to Rousseau or Teilhard de Chardin?
Wild berries of thorn-bushes and catkins of tamarisk.

Aerial view of the guelb-oasis of the boy
and herd, their habitat of old red sandstone.

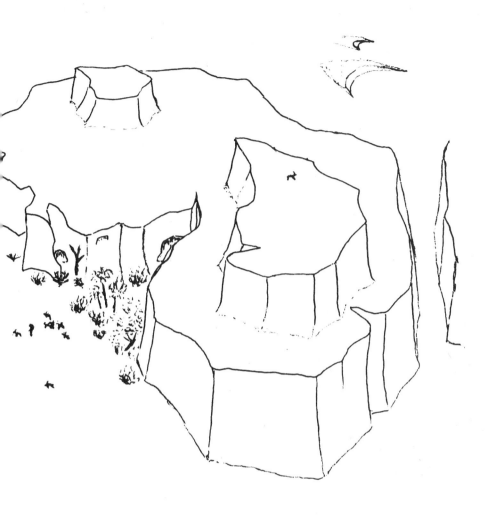

Where has the child learned to climb, a privilege beyond the physical powers of the gazelles? I have every reason to believe that the attraction of a bait or of some other objective will always induce any creature to invent the most unlikely expedients. In the same manner the child clambers up the vertical rock-face where, with a bite of his teeth, he cuts from the rock some kind of desert cabbage in a small compact ball, chewing the leathery leaves at length with a horizontal backward and forward movement of the jaws. (A few days later, as he yawns, I notice that the edges of his teeth are level, like those of a herviborous animal.) I myself attempt one of these impossible salads, but even chewing in the gazelle manner proves futile.

My strange climber, sometimes supported only by his big toe, quickly heaves himself on to a vertiginous winding track where some gazelles, who have come from behind across the plateau, move in single file; he starts to bolt jujubes from a *temen* (jujube-tree) overhanging the void below. Another day, he attacks the mauve catkins of the tall tamarisk and a swarm of sand-wasps takes to flight – he does not eat the catkins haphazardly, but leaves those which are not perfectly ripe, as if keeping them in reserve for a later 'visit'.

Jumping from branch to branch, his face and hair covered with gold-dust (the 'manna' of the ancient caravaneers of the deserts), my gazelle-boy finds his agility failing him for once: slipping on the smooth bark of one of the branches, he lands on an inconveniently placed thorn-bush which leaves him with numerous deep gashes. Immediately he begins to lick his wounds and continues to do so for some time, then makes for a little pocket of blue clay at the foot of the cliff-wall, licks the clay and spreads it on his gashes. (On another occasion, I see him smearing a wound caused by a sharp rock with the oozing, scented gum of a *talha* acacia, all with a great deal of licking – the Moorish nomads use this gum for the same purpose and so too, it seems, do the baboons of Asia.)

* * *

From time to time, one or several gazelles sniff at the child's hair, push their muzzles through it and even tug it with their teeth, giving little jerks of their heads. At such moments, a frenzied exchange of sniffs and licks takes place – the signs of acknowledgement and of affective communication constantly renewed. There follow little 'whisperings', a curious noise like that made by a goldfish as it surfaces in its bowl; the child, for his part, emits slow and gentle little cries from the back of the throat, without opening his mouth.

This 'kissing', almost ritual, takes place among groups of similar age and sex – and especially between the child and one particular old gazelle. Signs of this kind, clearly marks of affection, also circulate through the entire herd as if to allay mistrust and reinforce the cohesion of the group. (Some scholars, adopting the traditional Cartesian viewpoint, see this merely as a cleaning exercise, at least as far as the licking is concerned – but this is only valid when gazelles lick themselves!)

Now and again, one or two gazelles move round the child. Another sniffs at my hair and sometimes at the child's, then gives little licks, according to the mood of the moment.

On occasions, a male gazelle rubs his muzzle against the hindquarters of a female, scratches his flank against the trunk of a tamarisk (I never see the child doing this), or uses his horns to provoke a fellow-gazelle, who scampers off.

* * *

Every day brings new discoveries. The child, leaning over the water of the *guelta*, his pool, his hair over his eyes, stares at his face, as if admiring himself; eventually, he makes a comic attempt to catch his reflection, as if it were a stranger to him, by skimming the surface of the stagnant water with the back of his hand as he utters little piercing cries. A happy being lacking self-knowledge! (Already, I can see this causing a battle among philosophers and epistemologists, whether structuralists or not, tearing their hair or what is left of it – but I shall give them further food for thought!)

* * *

On one occasion, I surprise him, alone this time, performing a strange

43

dance, facing into the south wind, his eyes apparently shining with joy.

But, as the sun sinks, his face darkens, his features start to pucker, his expression grows heavy. As twilight falls, his whole body is overcome with prostration and eventually he crouches, motionless, under the neck of a large gazelle. This old female, which I notice more and more, with its shrivelled udders, eroded horns and a scar on its flank that also helps me to identify it, seems to have a particular predilection for the boy and the feeling is reciprocal: the licking, the rubbing of nose against muzzle and vice versa hardly ever ceases all day long – his old 'wet nurse' and adoptive mother?

* * *

One evening, seeing the child more exhausted than usual, an experiment occurs to me, rich in possibilities, but foolish and full of risk. Gathering some dead thorn-twigs, I quietly strike a match: a small flame begins to rise. The child, suddenly wide-awake, leaps back with an expression almost of terror, his eyelids fluttering.

Finally, as curiosity gets the better of fear, I see him slowly hold out a hand as if to catch the flames, now burning high. Then he starts to move round the fire, sometimes swaying on his feet, sometimes on all fours, drawing nearer in ever-decreasing circles, until finally he sniffs at the red embers. He grasps a fistful of embers and holds them for some time without apparent pain. Is it the hard callosities on his palms that enable him to achieve this feat? (Having seen men walk on fire in Greece, Ceylon and Tahiti, with different motivations, I feel the answer is not as simple as that.)

* * *

Living in closer and closer proximity to the child, even during the deepest hours of the night, I have another surprise: I see him suddenly upright, his neck stretched and chin jutting forward, strangely immobile – he is staring with large, ecstatic eyes at the full moon.

A moment later (following what signal?), he is off towards the horizon with great silent and elastic bounds, into the illuminated void of the night.

44

Immediate surroundings of the oasis-refuge.

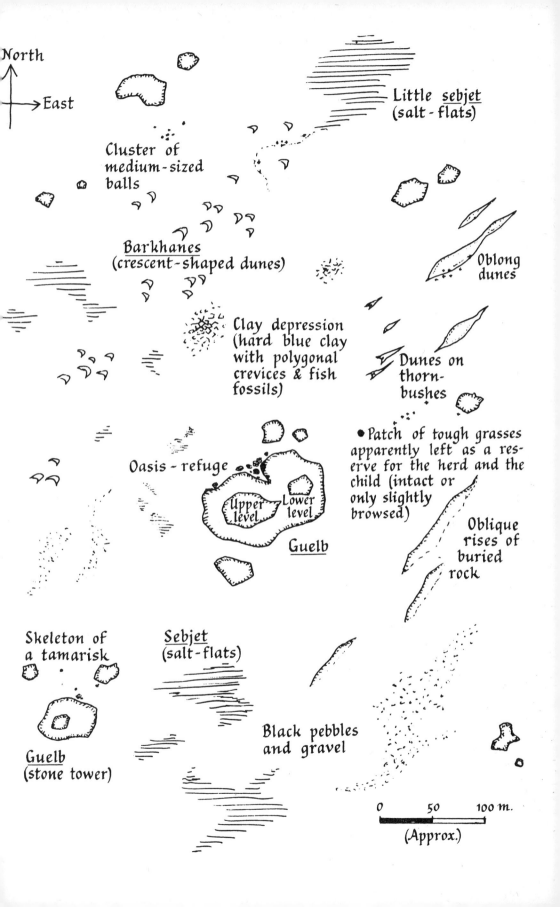

North

East

Little sebjet
(salt-flats)

Cluster of
medium-sized
balls

Oblong
dunes

Barkhanes
(crescent-shaped dunes)

Clay depression
(hard blue clay
with polygonal
crevices & fish
fossils)

Dunes on
thorn-
bushes

•Patch of tough grasses
apparently left as a res-
erve for the herd and the
child (intact or
only slightly
browsed)

Oasis-refuge

Oblique
rises of
buried
rock

Upper
level

Lower
level

Guelb

Skeleton of
a tamarisk

Sebjet
(salt-flats)

Guelb
(stone tower)

Black pebbles
and gravel

0   50   100 m.

(Approx.)

In the light of the moon, now high, he comes cantering back with his ghostly gazelles and I follow him into his nocturnal shelter. There, among the animals curling up to sleep, he does likewise, lying on his side, his head against his knees, as round as an egg on his litter of dead palm-leaves and palm fluff.

Sleeping close to the shelter (I still cannot endure the odour of animal-grease and ammonia, even when it is alleviated by the cool of the night), and opening an eye now and again to observe the child, I sometimes catch him twitching his ears, although he is apparently deep in sleep, or throwing out a leg in a movement of nervous relaxation obviously provoked by a dream or by spasms in the thigh-muscles. He even raises his head at the slightest unusual noise and sniffs around him with the tip of his feverish nose, his eyelids still half-closed. Beside him, his old 'nurse' does the same.

* * *

A week later, finally braving my bourgeois sense of smell, I resolve to spend a night in the child's shelter, on a new litter which I have laid there and which proves much warmer and more stable than an air-mattress. Under the arch of the rock-porch, half-naked in my short Nemdaï tunic (even after sniffing at it, the child has not been able to accept the strange fluffy chrysalid which these quaint Westerners wear at night), and my teeth chattering like an old piano, I muse on the catkins of the tall tamarisk dancing against the face of the moon, so absorbed that I forget that it is me living in this improbable universe.

Beneath the gazelles carved on the roof, a forest of horns rises; the murmurs and rumblings of the animals alternate with the airy fluting of tree-frogs (presumably) under the Star of the Prophet.

* * *

The violet dawn is ushered in by noises of eructations, flatulence and other graceful acts to which I became accustomed in the Moï huts of Central Viet-Nam and among the Indians of Amazonia.

46

*Quarters for the night: a cave with
Stone-Age symbols on the roof.*

An icy draught reaches me from the top of the cliff and from various holes, making me feel even more like a frozen mummy. The flies on the walls, hitherto immobile, begin to saunter slowly, becoming unbearable by midday.

Then an old male starts to move his horns, lifts his head, straightens his neck, rises, snorts and stamps his hoofs. The animals begin to dart out of the shelter, a few at a time, to lick the dew-drops forming in beads on the tips of leaves. The sound of their powerful inhalations on the damp sand (the child joining in) rises in strange unison as the first purple and violet cirrus clouds flood the sky.

As the sun appears once again between the high stone towers, the child and the herd move off into the first rays, like a beginning of the world, an airy shadow bathed in red-gold, the gazelles in rose-gold.

Later, I see him swaying again, then dancing with wild leaps and capers among his scattered gazelles, his expression more ecstatic than ever; he gives frenzied but almost inaudible little cries, the timbre of which unmistakably reveals extreme joy.

A climax is reached as all the joy, all the jubilant colours of the dawn, and the great organ drone of the sands (the dawn 'song' of the desert, of electro-static origin), finally draw from the boy the ghost of a smile, gone in a flash.

Many forms of human expression (tears, laughter, anger, etc.) charac-teristic of even the most primitive of men are unknown to this child, who has obviously been reared by animals. (In fact, the view that humanity 'expresses' itself by these manifestations is debatable: the Japanese or the Chinese hardly ever laugh or weep; people living in cold countries are known for their reserve. In general, the thresholds of pain and joy vary according to a person's conditioned attitude to life.)

* * *

The oasis seems to be a refuge for the child and his animals between long absences. Is it a permanent habitat? This is impossible to believe, seeing that gazelles migrate periodically.

The cave-shelter shows a cleanliness worthy of a Swiss or a Swedish

49

View from the rock-shelter by day.

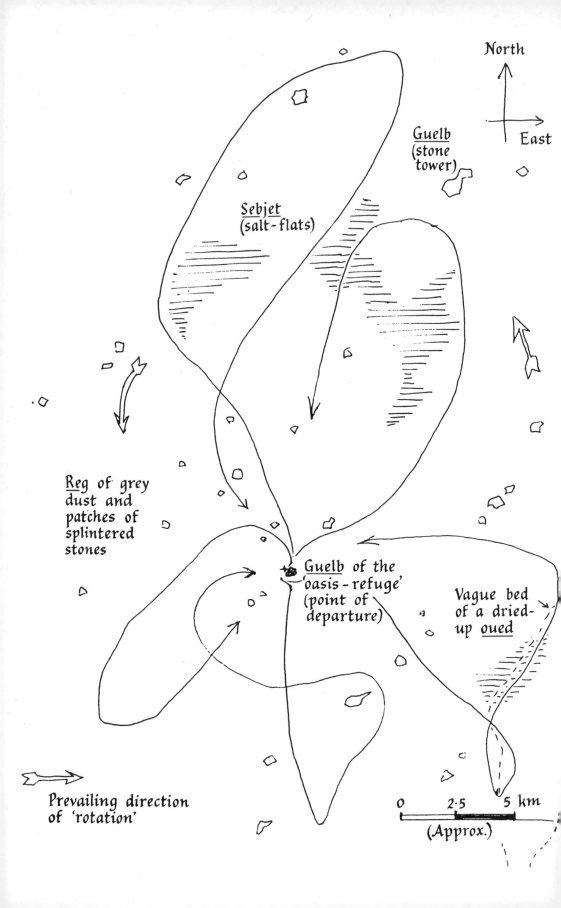

North

East

Guelb
(stone
tower)

Sebjet
(salt-flats)

Reg of grey
dust and
patches of
splintered
stones

Guelb of the
'oasis-refuge'
(point of
departure)

Vague bed
of a dried-
up oued

Prevailing direction
of 'rotation'

0   2·5   5 km

(Approx.)

apartment! Excrement has its appointed place at the back of the gorge; only the fawns allow themselves an occasional indulgence. At another point of the refuge area are the shells for delousing and 'dry-cleaning'; even the child uses them, carefully cleaning his hair on the shell with a backward and forward motion; then, tousled like a true Moor, he throws his hair back as a horse tosses its mane.

Why is it commonly assumed in Europe that wild children are necessarily dirty? Their chance 'educators' keep their own coats or feathers clean (like all wild animals and the majority of domestic animals). There are, admittedly, certain exceptional cases: children who live in total isolation or who have been abandoned to their own devices (congenital idiots or children who have been removed into isolation).

* * *

Pursuing my observation of the child's nocturnal life among his animals, and forcing myself to remain awake throughout the night so as not to miss anything, I discover the existence of an alternating rhythm of wakefulness and sleep, at intervals of roughly two to three hours. I follow some strange escapades in the depth of the night – gambollings, hunts for roots and fawns' games animating great shimmering expanses of salt in the light of the moon or the stars.

At these same late hours, I notice numerous little plants of the 'ephemeral' kind, pushing through crusts of salt, moist with dew, sprouting from the *sif* (ridge) of a few scattered dunes, growing between the pebbles or in the black dust of the *reg*, and even in the hexagonal crevices of the clay depressions. Here and there I find what look like roses of Jericho, strange moon-coloured flowers blossoming at ground-level.

Certain places are covered with weird flower-beds which appear for a single night – unreal, phantasmal little plants teeming with giant black coleoptera, scorpions that move mechanically and burrowing millipedes.

Here, the child and his animals browse together: the child on all fours, using his incisors but without pulling the plant up, his face against the ground and his hair falling into his eyes so that he cannot see; he maintains the same

51

Area covered by the short migrations (short cycle, two to three days).

position as he goes from one group of plants to another, sometimes only a few yards, sometimes several dozen yards away.

But the child never attacks the little fauna that roam his strange 'prairie', nor the lizards of the daytime. Like his tutors, he is herbivorous, except at rare moments when plant-life is lacking: then, with a certain reticence, he will munch an agama lizard, holding it by the tail, or a few worms extricated from under the bark of old wood.

6. THE BOY'S ORIGIN

Meanwhile, the intriguing problem of the 'all fours' and standing positions makes me feel that I must now attempt to resolve the child's probable origins.

Seeing him on his two legs almost as much as on all fours, I should imagine that he was 'abandoned' in the desert at the age of seven or eight months, having already learned something of the standing position. (A European child of the middle classes rarely attains this stage before one year, usually between a year and eighteen months, but the children of primitives and of nomads in general – little gipsies, for instance – are much more precocious in this and in other respects: the awakening of the sense-perceptions, practical intelligence, presence of mind, rapidity of reflexes and keenness of observation.)

Moorish children travel in baskets placed on the side of the camel. In all probability, this one of mine fell from a camel at the rear of a caravan, during the night (the torrid heat of the day would not have spared him). All it would have needed would have been a herd of migrating gazelles spending that same night in the vicinity, and a pregnant female in a nervous state or a female that had lost her fawn (through sickness or to a predatory jackal). It would be quite understandable that a compensatory instinct should then have come into play, just as hens which have lost their chicks sometimes rear ducks, or women without children of their own devote themselves to other people's or surround themselves with cats.

To complete the hypothesis: the well-known native habit of prolonged suckling by the mother (the phenomenon still exists in certain remote rural districts of Europe which have not yet been assailed by the tyrannical advertising of manufacturers of tinned and powdered milk) would explain why the child would still be at the suckling stage and also capable of the

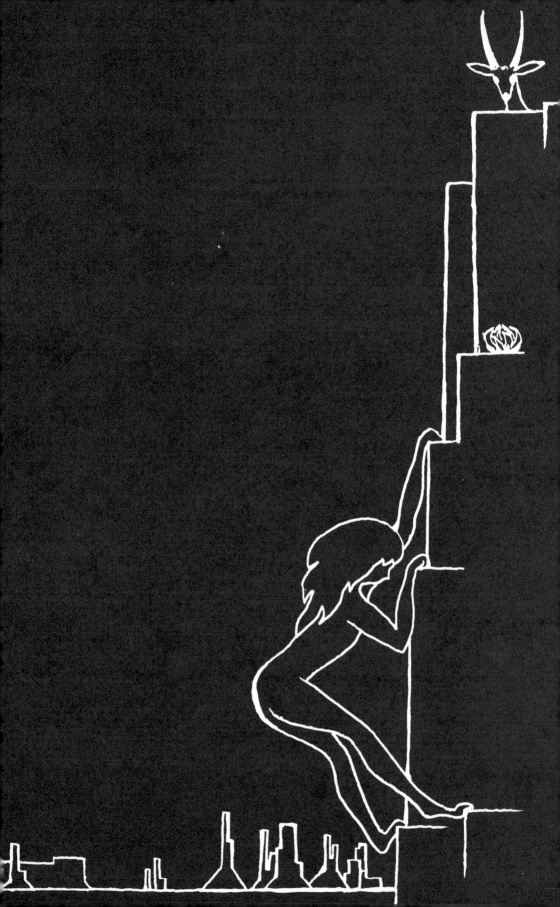

rapid mobility to which the gazelle would be accustomed (the young of a gazelle walk within twenty-four hours of being born).

'Deliberate abandonment' is the basic hypothesis of the French philosopher Lévi-Strauss: 'The majority of wild children are congenitally abnormal children who have been deliberately abandoned.' To this I would reply, in a relativist and pragmatic spirit, that there are only specific cases, wild children being too few in number for any kind of statistical analysis and, consequently, for a dogmatic *ex cathedra* definition.

I can say at once that I have not yet observed anything 'abnormal' in my gazelle-boy. His 'response' to his 'milieu' is adequate, a sign of normality in relation to his particular environment (normality in itself does not exist). Here, in such a rigorous setting – not to mention the hazard of fast-moving, undomesticated beasts – the slightest deviation would be punished with death and oblivion.

As for the child's ethnic origin, I should think him more likely to be a Nemdaï than a Moor, for his hair is not curly like that of the Moors; also, because of their way of life, there exists among the Nemadis a marked pre-adaptation to running; finally, their extremely poor and precarious existence gives them an affinity with the natural elements. (In India, nearly all wolf-children come from villages in forest clearings.)

Climbing the guelb *in search of rock-plants.*

Like a beginning of the world . . . ▶

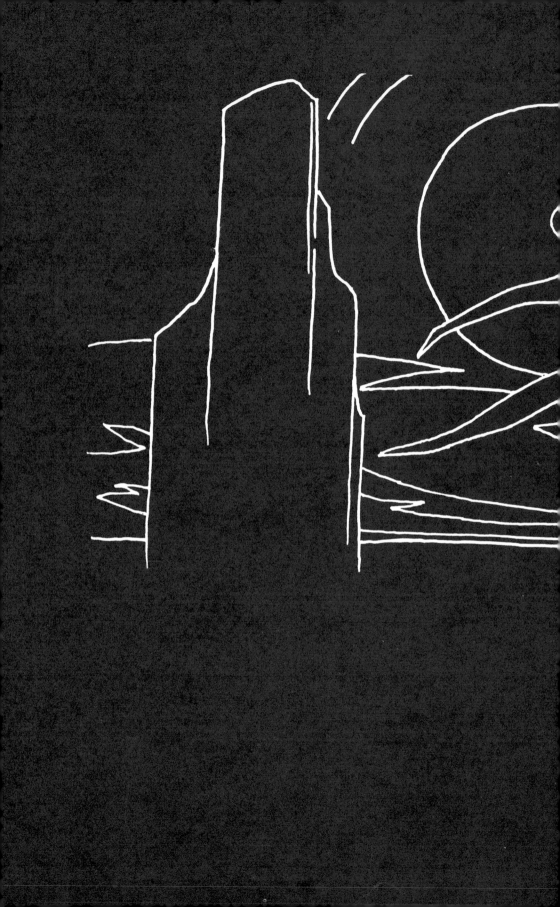

7. NOVEL METHODS OF COMMUNICATION

As the days pass in this rather unusual cohabitation, I become more interested in various possible modes of communication between myself and the child, between the child and the herd, and between the animals and myself – perhaps exchanges of a kind unforeseen and inconceivable in the present state of the human mind, especially the European mind which, in this technical age, is becoming increasingly alienated from the primary reflexes of communication and primitive 'participation' (in the sense in which the shamans understand the term).

* * *

To test the affective responses of the child, I try the experiment of a feigned departure.

When I return two days later, the child comes towards me with a crescendo of rapid little cries, clearly of joy (but still from the back of the throat), and licks me all over my body. His companions, some young gazelles, do likewise.

Later, like Ariadne with her first clew, I try to imitate the different timbres of the sounds made by the child (from the back of my throat). This kind of code, imitating that of the gazelles, resembles the system of bird-calls used (with or without decoy-birds) by hunters of waterfowl and which, if the imitation is perfect, almost invariably succeeds with any animal. In fact, the child always 'replies' adequately to my imitation: for example, my little cries from the back of the throat prompt in him the 'reflex' of giving me little licks all over my body. The system is obviously clear and simple, but is somewhat lacking in variety and scope.

* * *

58

Child and herd : hierarchical structure.

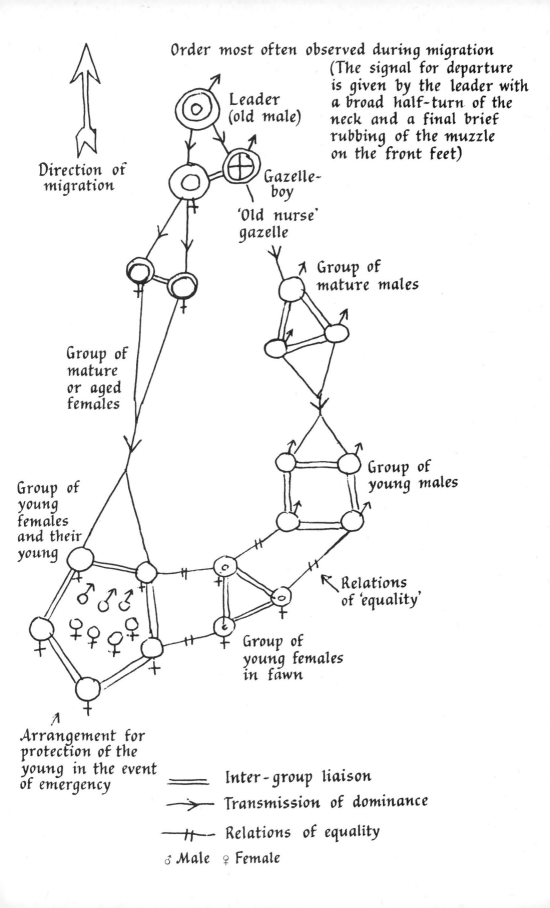

Direction of migration

Order most often observed during migration
(The signal for departure is given by the leader with a broad half-turn of the neck and a final brief rubbing of the muzzle on the front feet)

Leader (old male)

Gazelle-boy

'Old nurse' gazelle

Group of mature males

Group of mature or aged females

Group of young males

Group of young females and their young

Relations of 'equality'

Group of young females in fawn

♂ Male   ♀ Female

Arrangement for protection of the young in the event of emergency

——— Inter-group liaison

——➤ Transmission of dominance

——H— Relations of equality

♂ Male   ♀ Female

Still avoiding all explicit or articulated words (even in the child's presumed native language), which would be a futile procedure, I begin to experiment with some – and naturally those most adapted to his way of life – of the four hundred onomatopoeias and interjection-cries of the oldest prehistoric living language in Europe and possibly in the world: Euzkara, commonly known as Basque (I was myself born at the foot of the Atlantic Pyrenees).

We manage to exchange some four or five of these sound-signals (onomatopoeias and interjection-cries) without too much difficulty, but still from the back of the throat and with the mouth nearly always closed. In fact, these are simply variations of the child's ordinary repertoire of three cries of different timbres, which he has himself learned from his animals.

As regards this similarity of modes of communication among primitive beings, it would appear that the child has even arrived, by the path of 'abstraction' and not without some difficulty, at the stage of a single onomatopoeic noun, *kal*, meaning 'stone' or 'rock', the most universal of the human terms recognised as original by numerous linguists and students of semantics. But the child's voice, still emerging from the back of the throat and with lips barely opened, can utter only the sound *khah*. (To achieve this, I repeatedly hold up a stone, after putting my nose to it and pronouncing its 'prehistoric, name.)

The result obtained is clearly of limited significance. Nothing so far is comparable with the level of communication attained by the expression of the eyes. Indeed, is this not the most profound and least deceptive sign used by mankind anywhere on this earth?

The different expressions which the child's eyes assume, according to circumstances, can already be distinguished as representing joy, confidence, curiosity, pleasure, sadness, fright, uneasiness, desire, anxiety, ecstasy or utter bliss – qualitative manifestations which, to the despair of scientists, cannot be measured.

The only objection might be this: how has the boy come to experience the feelings which he appears to express? The 'languorous' eyes of his adoptive gazelles, almost expressionless in the monotony of their stare, are not remotely comparable.

Again, the child must have become accustomed, during the first few weeks of his life, to the expressions in the eyes of his natural mother (or, rather, those of the women of the nomad tribe generally, the so-called 'natural' mother being a limited phenomenon in time and in space).

* * *

Having exhausted the more or less classic methods of 'dialogue' and 'communication', and still somewhat unsatisfied, I sense the existence of a vast and little-explored 'no-man's-land'.

For the past two weeks it has seemed that certain movements made by the child and his animals answer and confirm one another, linking up in certain patterns. Signals are discernible, visual and conventional, as if codified in advance, and in which chance plays less and less part. A new and quite unforeseeable language which intrigues me more and more, repeated 'correspondences' to observe and a key that must be found so that they can be deciphered – a universe in itself, infinitely greater, simpler and more varied in its possibilities.

Having arrived at this point, I find some illuminating comparisons occurring to me. The Nemadis of Aguelt-en-Nemadi use coded signals when hunting gazelle and antelope, 'words-that-make-no-noise':

'I see some Dorcas gazelles': standing in profile, both arms raised sideways.

'I see some Addax antelopes': arms slightly raised, left hand turned back.

'I see some Biche-Robert gazelles': left arm and hand erect.

'Large herd of females': left arm and hand parallel to the ground.

'Stay there, females close by': right arm parallel to the ground, thumb downwards.

Of a similar kind are the codes of hand gestures used by the present-day aborigines of central Australia; the signs used by deaf-mutes; the 'esperanto', entirely dependent on gesture and gesticulation, used by the Redskins of North America at inter-tribal palavers. The Basque shepherds of my childhood often communicated solely by silent but eloquent gestures (what they called their 'signs-of-words-in-the-air').

At the extremes of the immense and diverse evolutionary chain of mind and being are the 'signa loquendi' of the Trappist Fathers (the monks whose

61

rule binds them to silence and who use only 'signs-for-speaking') and the coded 'information' which bees pass among themselves.

* * *

Having already had some experience of the diversity of living beings, and far from all intellectual taboos, I now seem to be grasping new modes of communication as I observe the child and his herd. One day, he goes off with them in search of new steppes of *drînn*, a grass usually dry and hard, but sometimes freshened and softened by a few drops of rain or dew. This is the beginning of a migration.

I manage to keep up with the child's trot, but not his gallop, which takes the form of gigantic leaps of three or four metres, just like his animals. Then I have to remount my camel and drive her hard. Escapades at this speed, worthy of a romantic painting, are fortunately of brief duration: my lips are rapidly chapped by a biting wind and the camel would not be able to keep up the pace.

From time to time, the child or one of the gazelles stops suddenly at a tuft of *drînn* and browses a juicy plant, then sets off again.

The roaming herd often takes advantage of the direction of the wind and its speed is thus increased. Sometimes managing to forge ahead on my mount, I stop on dazzling plains of salt, mirrors beneath the beating of the sun, where I see my companions flying like mirages.

There are other unexpected stops to unearth ball-shaped roots of *zila*, sweet and farinaceous. I even see the herd licking, with obvious pleasure, the patches of magnesian salt of the vast *sebkha*.

Again, the herd dashes off towards new ground and in new directions, sometimes deploying themselves in a fan-shaped formation, scattering to the four corners of the horizon, regrouping just as quickly, abruptly changing course at right-angles, like a shoal of fish; from afar I cannot see who is leading them.

Finally, bewildered by all these wild games, I have to admit defeat, like my camel.

* * *

62

System of the 'scouting' gazelle (observed at night during a general migration, nearly always for 'fields' of ephemeral plants).

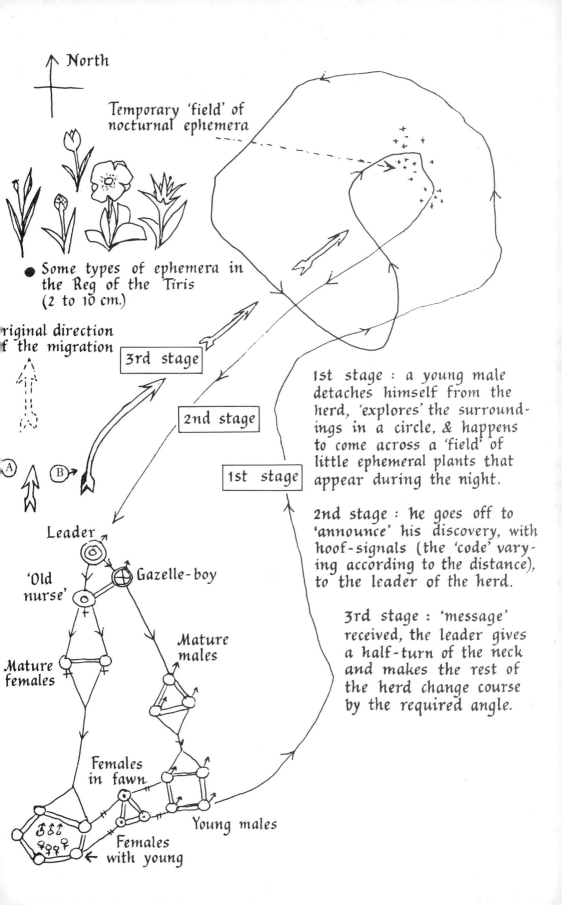

North

Temporary 'field' of
nocturnal ephemera

• Some types of ephemera in
the Reg of the Tiris
(2 to 10 cm.)

riginal direction
f the migration

3rd stage

2nd stage

1st stage

(A)   (B)

Leader

'Old
nurse'   Gazelle-boy

Mature
males

Mature
females

Females
in fawn

Young males

Females
with young

1st stage : a young male
detaches himself from the
herd, 'explores' the surroundings in a circle, & happens
to come across a 'field' of
little ephemeral plants that
appear during the night.

2nd stage : he goes off to
'announce' his discovery, with
hoof-signals (the 'code' varying according to the distance),
to the leader of the herd.

3rd stage : 'message'
received, the leader gives
a half-turn of the neck
and makes the rest of
the herd change course
by the required angle.

Awakening from a nap, after having collapsed at the feet of my camel, my head against the cracks of the salt, I now observe the child and his gazelles exchanging countless different signs and signals, obviously coded: stamping with the heels and hoofs, contortions of the neck, movements of the head, rhythmic motions of the tail, the ears, the horns, the wrists and fingers.

How am I to unravel all this? What is the key? My mind is increasingly exercised and stimulated by the question: where is the decoding key to be found? Will this be just another of the desert's mirages?

After several days of inertia, something 'clicks' in my mind as I see a gazelle suddenly detaching itself from the group, dashing off in an invisible streak, like a chameleon of the sands, and returning shortly afterwards, scratching the ground with two sharp movements of its left forefoot. Immediately the boy, to whom the signal seems to have been addressed, dashes off in the same direction as the animal.

Afraid that these might simply be two coincidental acts, I jump on to my camel and discover, about one kilometre away, a large desert 'anabasis' cabbage still green and with a mass of little sulphur-coloured flowers. The child is still there, attacking it with his incisors, even trying to uproot it with his hands.

Again I ask myself, is this just a coincidence? But gradually, going myself each time to verify these movements, I realise that the same code is always used for the same objective.

At last, I have discovered a first key!

* * *

Decoding this first signal of the hoofs enables me to decipher a dozen others of the same nature, varying according to the distance signalled:

Alternate stamping with the front hoofs: double the distance of the first (i.e. 2 km).

Alternate stamping of the front hoofs and then of the rear hoofs: triple the distance (3 km).

Simultaneous stamping of the front hoofs and then of the rear hoofs: four times the distance (about 5 km).

Stamping with diagonal movements of the hoofs: double the preceding distance (10 to 12 km).

Beyond this distance there are no more signs – this, it seems, is the beginning of infinity for a gazelle!

For distances under one kilometre:

Single stamp of the left front hoof: about 800 metres.

Single stamp of the right front hoof: about 500 metres.

Single stamp of the left rear hoof: 300–350 metres.

Jerk of the muzzle towards the back of the neck: all distances under 300 metres.

The 'message' is usually addressed to the leader of the herd, then to the pregnant females and to the females with young fawns, then to the child, and finally to the whole or to part of the rest of the herd. The 'messenger', nearly always a young male, takes up a position more or less in front of the animal or animals concerned, the length of his body often appearing to point in the direction of the food that has been located.

* * *

While making these observations, I also see a young female carrying in her mouth a tuft of *inîtî* or thorn-bush, still tender from the night and which she gives to her fawn. At the same time, I discover some strange leafless flowers which open out and close alternately in slow, rhythmic pulsations – a rare species, perhaps, which I must save *in extremis* from the mouth of a messenger-gazelle.

* * *

The child rarely takes the initiative in these coded signals. Sometimes I catch him giving a sudden little twist of the neck (an element of the code used to signal very short distances), stamping with his heels once or several times (if he is standing), scratching the ground with his hands or stretching out a leg (if he is on all fours), but I cannot yet determine what distances these signs represent.

My attention is now increasingly drawn to a new group of coded messages: my gazelle-boy is constantly miming signs with the muscles of his face, his scalp or his finger-tips, signs which, as before, nearly always correspond with (and occur almost simultaneously with) movements made by the herd with the tail, the ears, the horns and the head – probably a new silent language which may have nothing to do with the search for plants, a language for which I long to discover the key.

* * *

These apparent signals have nothing to do with the flies, an obvious explanation which for a long time I myself accepted: the same movements occur outside the hot hours of the day, when there are no flies to be seen.

The code-structure of this second series of signs is now discernible:

One movement induces another of the same kind from a neighbouring animal.

Two movements (usually with the ear or tail) prompt two more from the neighbour.

Two movements, a brief pause, two more, and a symmetrical response.

Then: two-one-two with a response of similar structure, and so on up to twelve.

Curiously, the 'system' seems to be based on a binary series forming multiple 'messages'.

The 'conversation', if I may use the term, thus passes in mysterious 'linear chains' through the herd (the child included), stops, starts again in another direction, and even forms intersections (with one or two circular chains).

Discovering the general pattern and even the dynamic structure of this strange new code still does not provide a key.

* * *

Towards the end of my first sojourn in this desert, other series of codes, more or less presumed on my part and independent of the first two series, are to prove even more obscure. Tantalising questions which always lead to other questions and never to answers. Bewildering!

I should at least like to solve the problems presented by the first series of signs. Who in the herd chooses the 'messenger' animal? The old 'patriarchal' male? Is there a special code to signify this choice? And so on.

8. WILD CAPERS

At the dawn on the *sebkha*, salt-flats of dewy sponge, among the scattered peaks of bronze gypsum and opal rock-salt, and in an icy wind (*chîchîlî*), the child and his animals embark on a new escapade, clearly the beginning of a great migration.

The herd pursues its wanderings across violet sands mingled with pebbles that flash like black mirrors, indulging in all manner of wild and dizzy games: this is El Meraïa, The Mirror, a sombre *reg* unmarked on maps where my companions run like white phantoms – here in the secret heart of the Tiris.

My feet are bleeding as I walk on these sharp-edged iridescent splinters. Mysterious shiny black balls roll into basins of purple-red clay. Fulgurites, tubes of vitrified sand formed by lightning, chink in the wind and sparkle like crystal amid the extreme intensity of this emptiness.

My gazelles trot and gallop in all directions, at ease in this hallucinating scenery, sometimes slackening their pace and performing little leaps like a bouncing ball; others chase black balls of *inîtî* thorn-bush which roll along in the wind, jumping over them and lifting their noses as migrating birds (storks? cranes?) pass overhead in long, airy formations against the burning sky.

Then come sands where mottled pebbles and pearls of banded agate sprout in a strange chaos of wondrous beauty, calling to mind another of my deserts in central Asia. I also discover a crater with a meteoric stone (I think) fallen from the stars and the sidereal void.

* * *

In the hottest hours of the day, columns of sand rise here and there, dancing and crackling with an electric hum, then subside. My senses of smell and hearing stretched to painful limits, and my skin tingling, I feel my

Torrid mid-day sun over the 'forbidden city', Reg of the Tiris.

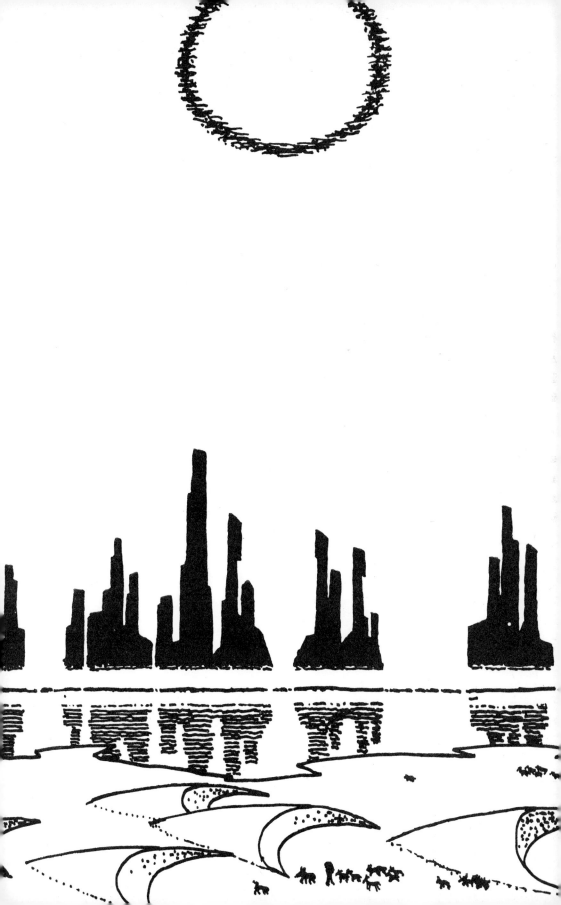

tentative way towards the full potentialities which exist at the very limits of freedom.

My tame fennec (which until now I have not allowed to mingle with the herd, in order not to complicate my observations) plays the fool with the gazelles, who threaten it with their horns.

The immense emptiness of the *reg* goes on and on, as though filling up the spaces between the islands of bare look-out towers hanging in mirages. And my gazelle-boy is like an elusive Ariel with his great pale gazelles in their windborne flight. The night finds them performing their giant leaps against the face of the nascent moon: what a marvel to see these chases indulged in for no reason, with not a jackal in sight, as if simply for the grace and pleasure of movement!

In the half-light of morning, chilled with dew, a little fawn has just been born; immediately its mother begins to lick it, cuts the umbilical cord, then chews and swallows the placenta. Gazelles and child come to acknowledge the little one with a touch of the muzzle or the nose: first the females of the mother's age-group, then the older females, then the males, the child and, finally, the leader of the herd.

* * *

A strange Christmas Eve. The *samun* (simoon), the 'wind of poison', rages across the sky. The sun, turning a reddish amber, is crowned with a halo of blood. Scorpions with nippers appear from all directions. Electric hummings crackle all around.

The skeleton of a large Addax antelope is blown about, its eye-sockets empty and its ribs in the air. Balls of thorn-bush roll along furiously. There are wild gleams and flashes, like St. Elmo's fire or sinister phosphenes, mingled with curious violet half-moons.

In this parching desert storm, my vagabond herd assembles as quickly as possible, huddling together, motionless before the unchained elements, the child's hair mingling with the horns.

After this infernal *harmattan* my lips are cracked, my body covered with cracks and blisters despite the palm-oil, and my provisions are almost at an

71

Games among the thorn-bushes and the heat columns;
El Meraïa, Reg of the Tiris.

*El Meraïa : the migrating herd on
the sun-dazzled salt-flats.*

end despite stringent economies: a shadow of myself, surviving only by my passion for the child and his gazelles. How long shall I have to continue like this?

* * *

During a delousing session, a gazelle leaps over the child, who is smothered in powdery clay. These leaps now seem to become more frequent, apparently because of the relative abundance of tufts of *drînn* in this corner of the *reg*.

The following dawn, the strange spontaneous games of the previous day grow more intense, assuming the form of alternating 'leap-frog' movements. This cavalcade for two becomes a cavalcade for four and then, at moments, a bizarre merry-go-round with two or three concentric circles of swirling animals. Certain gazelles, jumping high into the air, their legs spread out rigidly, seem to set the rhythm – an improbable display of acrobatics in which the child takes part, leaping round with the gazelles.

'Akhou', my fennec, whirls round the frenzied group. Gripped, in spite of myself, by the magic of this moment of supreme purity and freedom, I find myself being drawn into the carousel.

At night, the same strange merry-making, a ghostly, dream-like dance joined now by the frantic capers of the jerboas.

The 'merry-go-round'.

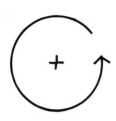

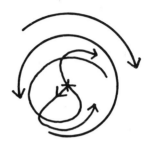

I. Initial stage: one 'player' turning round another, stationary player (either the child or a gazelle); the most common formation, not always leading to the full development.

IV. Fourth stage: the stationary player, once jumped over, then crosses over the jumper in turn. Another player joins in, forming an outer circle.

II. Second stage: two partners revolve in opposite directions.

III. Third stage: the first partner breaks his circle and jumps over the stationary player.

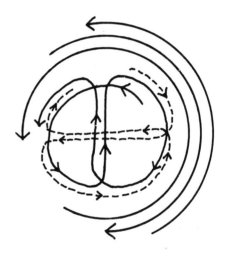

V. Final stage: the central intercrossing assumes the form of a 'solar cross'. On the periphery, other circles of players form until all the animals are involved and exhaustion is reached.

The strange development of the 'merry-go-round'.
The central intercrossing takes the form of
alternate leap-frog movements.

The leap-frog.

9. EPILOGUE TO THE FIRST ENCOUNTER

Elevated by the discovery of a new universe, I no longer feel my human limitations, like the yogis of the Himalayas who go about in the glistening snow with empty bellies and bare feet and bodies – it is an uncanny liberation of the heart, the body and the mind in this 'fabulous opera' reminiscent of Rimbaud or of the pilgrims of Katmandu who have tried to break down all the absurd walls of existence.

But the end of this life which I have been living at the boundaries of unreality comes suddenly as the herd takes to flight and vanishes over the immense horizon. What has happened? My gazelle-boy and his herd must have caught the scent of a jackal or of a caravan of R'Gueïbat Moors or other nomads.

Immediately, my nerves give way. A painful paralysis transfixes me. But terror at the thought of leaving my bones here enables me to summon my last remaining strength. In fact, after a few hours' march, I find the fresh traces of a caravan, droppings included, in the dust of the *reg*.

At the limits of hunger and, above all, thirst, I have somehow reached safety.

* * *

This last migration of the child and his animals already seems to have a direction and a pattern. All these movements from oasis to stamping-ground, and then to more distant stamping-grounds, appear to take the form of mysterious 'rotations', 'quarter' by 'quarter', as if to allow the meagre vegetation time to grow again.

Perhaps there are even migrations to far-distant parts, following the cycle of the rains, a necessary rhythm for everything that lives in the desert? But, to discover the existence of such a rhythm, I should have to live here for a whole year.

Area covered by the great migrations (based on observation of three great migrations).

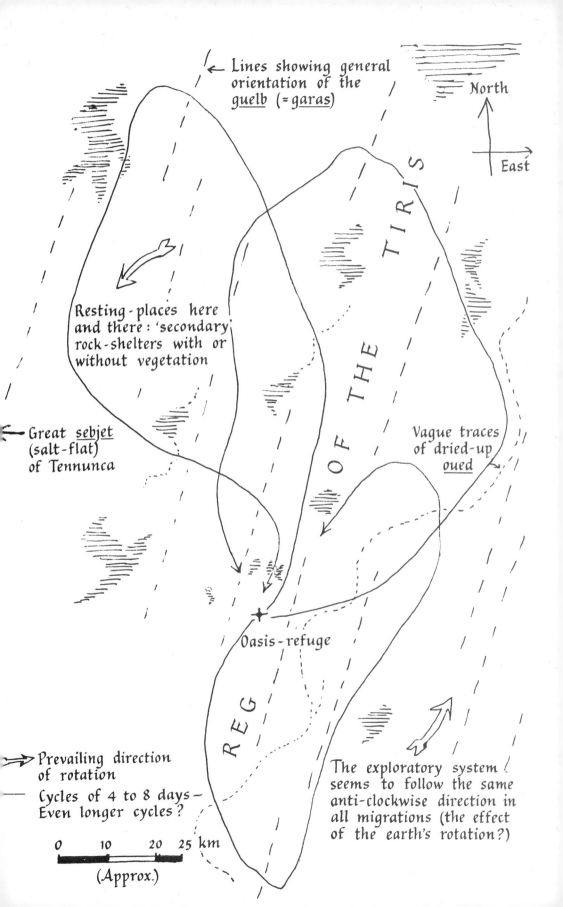

Lines showing general orientation of the guelb (= garas)

North

East

TIRIS

OF THE

Resting-places here and there: 'secondary rock-shelters with or without vegetation

← Great sebjet (salt-flat) of Tennunca

Vague traces of dried-up oued →

Oasis-refuge

REG

⇒ Prevailing direction of rotation

— Cycles of 4 to 8 days — Even longer cycles?

The exploratory system seems to follow the same anti-clockwise direction in all migrations (the effect of the earth's rotation?)

0   10   20 25 km

(Approx.)

10. THE SECOND ENCOUNTER

On my return to the Basque country, I related my discovery to Professor Théodore Monod, my former 'boss' at the Institut Français d'Afrique Noire at Dakar, who published a summary of our correspondence (simply to establish dates) in the Institute's journal, *Notes africaines*. We agreed not to let this discovery become generally known, for what was at stake was the safety of a creature still too fragile to defend himself against the enterprises of men, well-intentioned or otherwise.

Two years later, in 1963, again with my own limited resources, I set off once more, this time through southern Morocco. (My first expedition, in 1960-1, started from a Basque tunny-boat calling at Port-Etienne.)

On my journey I received unexpected assistance from a captain-instructor of the Cercle Militaire Français of El Aioudj-Idjil (formerly French Mauritania). Since my first expedition, the restrictions on entry to the Spanish Rio de Oro had been slightly relaxed.

The captain, intrigued by the story of my first extraordinary discovery – like his inseparable aide-de-camp – wanted to see for himself. The condition on which I insisted in committing this first indiscretion was that the whole affair should be regarded as a 'military secret'.

A few days later, the three of us were travelling by jeep towards our destination. Without saying anything, I felt a heavy anguish growing within me at the thought of not finding the child alive (a victim of the jackals that roam the desert), or of having to spend days and days painstakingly following the traces of the herd's migrations if the boy and his gazelles were not to be found at their main refuge. (Also, there would be much less time available for searching, because of the jeep's rapid fuel-consumption due to evaporation – a drawback not presented by my brave old 'desert ship', my indefatigable camel.)

* * *

About two *griyb* ('two hours of walking following the lie of the land') from the oasis, which I manage to find with some difficulty, I ask my companions to leave the vehicle there so as not to frighten the child with the smell of petrol and the noise of the engine, and I also ask them not to come too near, but to be content to observe from a distance with their ship's binoculars, perhaps from the top of a *guelb*.

When we reach the agreed point, I continue alone. I am in luck, for I soon find the child, this time in his oasis-refuge. On all fours behind his thorn-bushes and dense shrubs of euphorbia, he is more developed, his muscles stronger and firmer, his face more hollow and less round; but the pubic hair still has the characteristics of childhood, and so I presume that he has not yet reached puberty. His herd does not look quite the same: some gazelles seem to have disappeared (unless they are behind the rock), while others have grown.

I repeat the 'taming' technique of our first encounter, at the same time drawing on my experience of all the subtle variety of codes. After only a few hours, the child and his gazelles 'recognise' me in the same manner as before. This time, after my long absence, the affective signals of the little licks of the tongue are not particularly demonstrative. (Forgetfulness? – but what is memory in the case of a wild child? Is it simply a practical 'memorising' for the purposes of survival, as in his animal-mentors?)

* * *

Since my first visit, new clumps of crimson and silver bushes have grown in the oasis-refuge. Everything seems once again to breathe freedom and lightness.

Despite the torrid heat of this late season, the oozing *guelta* in the hollow of the cliff now flows in a continuous trickle. This phenomenon, which defies all logic, is probably due to the source being a 'condenser', one of many to be found in the desert. Without it neither the oasis nor the child, it seems, would survive the hottest part of the summer. Although the origins of the phenomenon long remained a mystery, its existence has been known to all nomads from time immemorial. Its secret lies in the humidity of the air condensing

in unstable droplets, which form along the faces of underground fissures and sometimes, as the result of an earth-tremor or some other shock, merge in sudden jets. (In the *Reg* of the Ténéré, at the foot of a tower of smooth, fissured sandstone, I remember seeing a Targui nomad striking the rock-face with a large stone. After several blows a spring gushed forth, filling the *guerbas* – water-skins – which had been carefully placed to collect the water. As it emptied, the spring gradually dwindled and then resumed its almost invisible oozing. These unorthodox water-holes, which are never mentioned on the maps produced by the Western world, are marked with prehistoric signs carved on the adjacent rock-face. These mysterious 'condensers' were used at Constantinople in the reign of Theodosius and for several centuries saved the city from the Turkish invasion – but these were artificial condensers, formed by piling up stones haphazardly in dozens of high pyramids. Recently, I learned that the Israelis used to construct similar piles of stones to water their plantations in the Negev desert.)

* * *

The presence of the captain and his aide-de-camp, a few miles away, seems to inspire a certain fear in the child and his animals and to restrict the spontaneity of their frolics.

Having learned something of the reactions of wild children in general since my first expedition, and thus mentally prepared for possible new developments, I soon find myself making progress with the multiple signals of the second series of codes used by the child and his animals, though the key still eludes me.

First of all, a 'hierarchy' is discernible. The signal of the tail, the ears or the twist of the neck usually passes from the oldest animal – the leader of the group – to the child, then to the others in descending order of seniority, the young females and their little ones being the last in the chain.

I notice that the child's old female 'nurse' has disappeared: two years have passed since my first stay. The child does not seem to have been affected either in his behaviour or in his health; the herd of animals must have served him as a substitute, a large adopted 'family' of the kind found among the old

83

Between salt-flats and towers.

nobility, the nomads, the gipsies and all primitive peoples living a tribal existence (and now the hippies!). 'Maternal frustration', animal or human, is a quite recent and geographically limited idea – as a dyed-in-the-wool Marxist would say, a bourgeois idea and not an ontological fact.

* * *

The signals continue to circulate between the boy and his gazelles, then among the gazelles; that the signals mean something becomes increasingly clear – but what do they mean?

Absorbed in my thoughts, I fail to notice the gazelle-leader's 'hierarchic warning signal' and receive a well-placed butt on my hind-quarters. Inadvertently I had made the mistake of placing myself in front of the little herd.

Immediately, like the blow with the stick used by the master of Zen for the 'illumination' of his disciple, the motivation of the second series of signals, or at least some of them, becomes clear: odours. Even in the desert, odours of all sorts exist for a nose trained from birth to recognise them.

Now that I have found the right thread-end, the skein begins to untangle itself, starting with certain plants of a particularly odoriferous kind. The signal indicating the kind of odour is given by a swish of the tail on the part of the animal that has first scented it with quivering nostrils; the animal then transmits the 'information' in the direction of 'ascending hierarchy' and it finally reaches the leader. The signal is then passed down again to the first animal, which immediately scampers off towards the source of the odour.

This latter code sometimes overlaps with the first series of codes, which hardly helps to clarify the system as a whole.

* * *

Other coded variants are revealed in the course of curious little escapades round the oasis-refuge. Here is one example:

A young male gazelle detaches itself from its sex- and age-group and, taking a circular route, 'explores' an area far ahead of the rest of the herd.

84

At night, the objective is often a 'field' of ephemeral plants. The animal returns to announce the news to the leader with the customary stamping of the hoofs (the number of stamps varying according to the distance).

'Message received', the leader, with a sharp half-turn of his neck, makes the rest of the herd change course by the appropriate angle.

* * *

In both systems of codes, I observe the determining role of the gazelle-leader and his tail-signal indicating 'permission granted'.

By the same process of thought I realise, somewhat belatedly, that the child is not as free as I had believed and that he too has to conform to the social pattern. If he were to show dissent, a butt of the horns would promptly send him flying on to the sand! At first I had imagined him totally free *à la* Rousseau – but he is under an obligation: without his adoptive herd he would not have survived alone in the desert.

* * *

The relatively short time granted me by the captain and his aide (the military are always in a hurry) allows me only a few furtive soundings and I have to make sure that my companions do not find themselves to windward of the child and his herd – otherwise, there would be a frantic flight. Luckily, the *harmattan* blowing steadily from the north-east enables me to avoid being caught unawares. In the meantime, periods of immobility enable me to hear the whisper-like murmurings of these delightful animals and to observe them indulging their whimsical little gestures of the hoofs and muzzle which, at moments such as these, do not belong to any systematic code.

* * *

A second group of odours soon becomes evident, signalled with the ears and, it seems, by the same hierarchic routes: the smell of a passing fennec, which eventually reached even my civilised nose, then that of an Addax

85

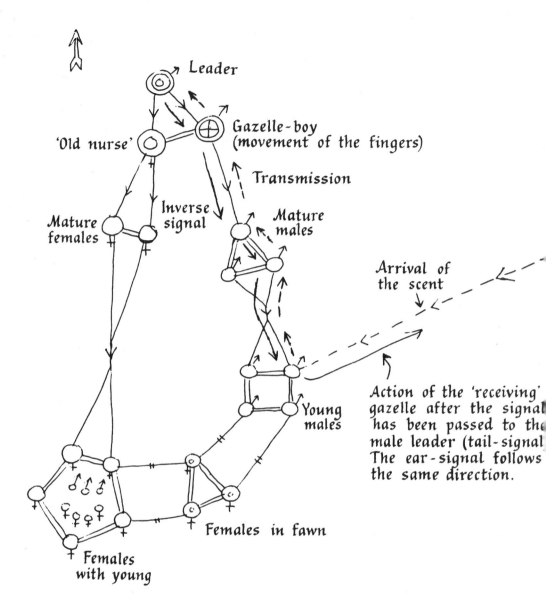

Leader

Gazelle-boy
(movement of the fingers)

'Old nurse'

Transmission

Inverse
signal

Mature
females

Mature
males

Arrival of
the scent

Young
males

Action of the 'receiving'
gazelle after the signal
has been passed to the
male leader (tail-signal)
The ear-signal follows
the same direction.

Females in fawn

Females
with young

antelope trespassing on foreign territory, the smell of a Dorcas gazelle, a jackal or a hyena.

Signalling with the ears appears to be reserved for warnings that unusual or dangerous creatures are in the vicinity.

* * *

Other groups or 'families' of signals pose problems and once again I find myself bewildered. Even the question of the structures based on binary multiplication, which I observed during my first stay, would require weeks for a detailed analysis (evaluation of distance, intensity, etc.).

However, I observe that the leader has a certain way of turning the neck in a semi-circle, which is always a signal to move off again, to begin a migration or possibly even to take to flight, after a signal has been received from a gazelle on look-out duty.

Finally, I notice that a certain movement of the child's fingers, like a nervous tic, corresponds more precisely with the chain of tail-movements made by his animals; his facial movements, the rictus of the cheek-bones and the twitching of the scalp, correspond to the chain of ear-signals of his animals (the child's own ears are always hidden under his mop of hair).

* * *

In the latter phases of my solitude with the child and his herd I notice, though rather belatedly, a habit of frequently sniffing at prints in the sand, the clay or the salt: prints of birds, jackals, fennecs, lizards, Addax antelopes or Dorcas gazelles. A fresh track, or one that has only just been discovered, prompts a signal of the ears (or of the scalp in the case of the child) and the familiar process of transmission begins again.

The excreta scattered here and there along these tracks are sniffed with varying degrees of curiosity, according to their whiteness or their smoothness (caused by the desert wind), and prompt the same ritual of transmission.

* * *

87

Communication on the basis of hierarchical structure.

A *sirli*, high in the sky and motionless, makes a shrilly modulated whistling sound, as if giving a final warning signal. Immediately, the gazelles close up, some of them making as if to challenge an invisible enemy with an array of horns.

As the first star appears in the west, and with no more signals from the *sirli*, the herd and child relax again in the mauve and bronze light of the sun's last rays. At the edge of the flowering bushes of the oasis, under the great tamarisk where bats with their strident little cries and heavy, glittering beetles flitter about, the child and gazelles, bathed in light, almost immobile, slowly exchange sniffs of the nose and muzzle in the warm eternity of the evening.

* * *

Towards the end of this second but brief sojourn in this desert, my captain and his aide join me so that they can carry out their own scientific observations at closer quarters – but, as I expected, their efforts prove futile.

In the jeep we follow the herd's traces and manage to catch sight of the little group, like a mirage, in the copper light of the setting sun. As a last resort, the captain, determined at least to ascertain the maximum speed of the child when forced to run at his fastest, puts his foot down hard on the accelerator and gradually overtakes him. Following close behind the child, we observe him reaching a speed of 52–54 km/h with gigantic, continuous leaps about four metres in length, like his gazelles. This must be what happens when fear of a jackal or a hyena is communicated to the herd.

For the briefest of moments, the child and his animals find themselves forced into a straight line as they run in front of the jeep between the high walls of two *guelb*. Until this moment, the child and his gazelles have taken a sly delight in zigzagging in all directions, as if to shake off their pursuers. Alas, the captain, seized by the competitive enthusiasm peculiar to the military and to sportsmen, wants to continue the chase to see if 'the child can beat his own record' (!). I shout at him to stop, but I am wasting my time! Then a well-timed puncture tosses all of us out, arms and baggage included, on to the stones of the *reg*. The captain attempts other stupidities, trying to

88

capture the child, but I stop him just in time by seizing the jeep's controls. I prefer to say no more about this part of the story, which belongs to the world of Westerns and comic strips.

I feel a deep sadness at leaving the child in this manner, with the vision of a desperate flight – beautiful none the less, almost unreal – into the dazzling immensity of the *reg*.

The 'forbidden city' : stone organ-pipes and heat mist. ▶

PART TWO

11. RECENT DEVELOPMENTS

In spite of my deliberate silence about the gazelle-boy of the Spanish Sahara, an attempt to capture him was made in 1966 by some American officers of the NATO base of Villa Cisneros in the Rio de Oro, who flew all over the Tiris searching for him (no precise map-references or place-names had been published). Having spotted him in the course of a migration with his herd, the American officers returned almost immediately with two helicopters to which a net was fixed in the hope that, by dragging it along the ground, they would be able to capture the child alive. Fortunately, despite repeated attempts, they did not succeed. (This information was supplied to me by Sidi Krokhtar Ould Harmi, a nomad teacher.)

Their failure was only to be expected. All this noisy, clumsy and cumbersome deployment of machinery, so typically American, would merely give the child and his animals, so keen of sight and hearing, ample time to find an invisible refuge in the black shadows of a *guelb* or a rock-shelter, especially since the flights were made mostly at night.

Quite apart from the traumatic effects of such a brutally inhuman method of capture, it is an established fact that wild children are not 'readaptable' once they have passed the age of three or four.

Professor Monod and myself agreed at the outset to leave the gazelle-boy of the Rio de Oro to live in freedom with his gazelles, especially since I had been struck by the equilibrium of his existence in the purity of those great open spaces. To make the child a candidate for our producer–consumer civilisation, dressing him in lounge-suit and tie or in dungarees (or condemning him to stagnation in some home for deaf-mutes or idiot children), at a time when an increasingly large proportion of the younger generation is rejecting the 'values' of our Western civilisation, would be senseless!

Moreover, all the studies made of children of this kind, in recent and in earlier times, have been concerned only with captive children, broken-down

93

guinea-pigs from whom the most insignificant results have been obtained by methods that have been almost invariably inadequate and ill-adapted, not to say absurd and even inhuman.

Even Professor Itard (1774–1838), a French scholar in advance of his time and the inspired precursor of all contemporary education, a man of heart influenced by the liberal, naturalist ideas of Jean-Jacques Rousseau, was not able to make his wild child, Victor of Aveyron, a true human being, nor was he able to give him back the happiness which, however relative, had been his to enjoy in the rugged plateaus of Rouergue.

One might as well study the life of a beast in a cage – those wretched animals swaying like automata all day long, just like prisoners in solitary confinement or wild children who have been subjected to similar conditions.

A second attempt to capture the gazelle-boy was made by the same Americans of Villa Cisneros in June–July 1970, at the time when this book was being written. When I was in Geneva for some lectures, the explorer Paul Lambert, well-known for his films and books on the Indians of South America and other parts of the world, told me the sad news that another attempt was imminent – immediately, I moved heaven and earth to protect the child and alerted the appropriate persons.

I now have every reason to believe that the danger is past. If the attempt had succeeded, every American in deepest Texas would have seen the child on his little screen, stuffed with tranquillisers and, on his arm, a Hollywood-style native girl darkened with sun-tan, between advertisements for hot dogs and biological washing-powders.

One thing would have consoled me: the Hippies of the New World, living in their communes amid Nature, would surely have made the child their archetype, along with Thoreau (the man of the woods), Marcuse and Saint Francis of Assisi.

* * *

In the course of my two sojourns with the wild child and his gazelles, the child 'taught' me, above all, certain spontaneous states of soul, states of the utmost purity and freedom before the elements: privileged moments, as it

94

were eternity itself, like those attained by Zen in the Far East and by the Hindu sage, Krishnamurti, the most deconditioned of human beings; intuitive states, sensitive and even sensualist, recently rediscovered by the best of the Hippies; a kind of instinctive primary osmosis (this unconscious intelligence) with the great elemental forces of Nature attained, without the intervention of any human or animal educator, at the most receptive and 'transparent' age.

How, then, could a 'nature-child' (in every sense of the term) be *himself* in an environment prefabricated by Man, who imposes his own conventional and arbitrary conceptual 'elements'?

The truth is this: the influence of nineteenth- and twentieth-century Western man (with a small *m* – and woman also?), who has been living on mental stereotypes of Judaeo-Christian origin, must be reduced.

The Moors and the Nemadis, for instance, look on my wild child as a *jinnee* of the desert, facetious and benevolent. The Hindus see their wolf-children as reincarnations of Krishna, the god-child playing the flute and crowned with leaves.

Thus, in my innermost self, the wild child whom I discovered by chance has unexpectedly become, as it were, the point of convergence of my long and obscure 'quest' for fulfilment across five continents.

'. . . The shell murmurs and always will murmur for the one who alone knows and wants to hear': a Polynesian proverb which the reader must interpret for himself!

COMPARATIVE ANALYSIS OF THE 'CULTURAL' AND SENSORY ACQUISITIONS OF THE CHILD

From the gazelles

Climbing rocks and the stone towers.

Keen sense of smell.

Sniffing the wind in the same manner as these ungulates (neck stretched, nose puckered).

Far-sightedness (though this is also characteristic of nomads).

Coded signals with the hands, feet, nose and scalp.

Great speed.

Giant bounds (running and standing). Great leaps over obstacles.

Various games peculiar to these animals.

Binary rhythmic evaluation in use of coded signals.

Delousing and degreasing with clayey shells.

Short, irregular rhythms of sleep.

'All fours' position (for about one quarter of the time) with great running speed in this position.

Participation in the herd-group and in its gazelle-style hierarchy.

Licking wounds and covering them with gum and clay.

Nose-to-nose sniffing (recognition) and licking (affective communication).

Licking of the nocturnal dew and of the surface of the water (lapping).

Exclusively herbivorous (seeds, roots, leaves, fruit), except in extreme circumstances. Slow mastication.
Marking common territory in the mammalian manner (excreta).

Orientation (in the manner of animals of steppe regions).

From his human origin

(Before his 'adoption' by the gazelles, making it possible to estimate the minimum limit of 'rupture' at 5–7 months – i.e. for a nomad child.)

Standing position (for about three-quarters of the time).

Expressive look and mobility of the eyes (special attention paid to the elements, a common phenomenon among nomads).

Litter for the night shelter (probably a throw-back to the cushions or the goatskins of the mother-tent).

Thumb-sucking (probably a sudden weaning from the gazelle-nurse, for the gazelle has a short sexual cycle; and a first, temporary weaning on the transition from the human to the animal state).

THE INDETERMINABLE

Sleeping in a ball (psychoanalysts see this as a frustration of the 'first state', the state preceding the rupture with the human nomad group).

Climbing date-palms and other trees: the desire to reach a bait suspended in the air will induce a monkey to pile boxes one on top of another – in the case of the child, a similarity can be seen in his climbing up rocks.

Apparent insensitivity to the cold of the night. But nomad children, who are traditionally naked until puberty (like the gipsies of Europe), do not seem to suffer from the cold; they rarely catch colds or other broncho-pulmonary maladies.

The use of clay is perhaps debatable, for nomads and hunting peoples nearly always use it as a medication.

Numerous vague little details concerning the character of the child, the heredity (unknown) of his genetic family, and his physiological type.

CONCLUSION

The earlier the child assumed this 'gazelle life', the greater would be the process of imitation or 'gazelle acculturation'. The same would apply to any animal, according to its level of evolution. But one would need a dozen of these children, living in the same conditions, to draw any hard and fast conclusions.

12. ON CHILDREN REARED BY ANIMALS

A recently published work, *Les Enfants sauvages* by Lucien Malson, reveals that fifty-three wild children (also called, improperly and misleadingly, 'wolf-children') have been found in different countries since the year 1344. The animal 'nurses' or 'tutors', in addition to the classic wolf, include panthers, bears, leopards and monkeys. There are also cases of children who appear to have grown up alone in a natural environment, among them the famous Victor of Aveyron.

My gazelle-boy appears last-but-one in the book's central list of wild children, just before the monkey-child of Teheran. But the latter has just been dethroned, as I write this book, by a couple of wild children found in Lebanon in October 1970.

But it seems that, up to the present time, I am alone in having lived with one of these children in its original environment. This is due to no special merit on my part: why this frantic urge to capture wild children as soon as they are discovered, instead of observing them in their own environment, at least for a time?

There is, moreover, only one other known case of a wild child adopted by gazelles, though once again the child was not observed at length and the discovery was not made known until the day of his capture. (André Demaison, *Le Livre des enfants sauvages*, ed. A. Bonne, Paris, and various secondary sources.)

In 1946 a wild child was discovered in Syria, with some gazelles, a boy apparently twelve to thirteen years old whose galloping leaps enabled him to move as quickly as his animals. It was possible to follow the running child through binoculars, but he was caught only after being chased by an Iraqi army jeep. Though he managed to maintain a speed of 50 km/h, he was eventually captured and shamefully bound hand and foot. Tall and slender, with a bushy mop of black hair, powerful ankles and muscles like steel springs, the boy resembled the youths of the Koniagui tribe in Upper Gambia, who hunt with bows and run as fast as their dogs, forcing hares and even antelopes to run for their lives. The child was then entrusted to the care of peasants, who never managed to prevent his constant breaks for freedom. Still alive in 1955, he was taken into the charge of the country's public assistance authorities, but he proved refractory to all education. In the course of yet another and quite spectacular attempt to escape, he jumped from one of the first-floor windows of the establishment, spreading panic in the streets of Damascus with his giant bounds; it seems that his 'educators' had no hesitation in subjecting him to a sinister and revolting surgical operation, in which the Achilles tendons were mutilated to prevent him making further attempts to escape.

I learned of this case in 1965, from the book by André Demaison, *Le Livre des enfants sauvages*. Later, I began searching for possible documentary evidence of the child's appearance, but in vain. I have every reason to believe that this remarkable runner must have had a long and slender body, with rigid muscles like springs, since it is a law of nature that physical similarities coincide with similarities of function. Herbivorous like my gazelle-boy, he must also have had a peaceful, attractive countenance, not like that of wolf-children.

Certain persons, confusing truths of observation with the Cartesian approach, think that I idealise and interpret too much according to my own fancies in emphasising the intuitive and 'contemplative' attitudes of my gazelle-boy before the great elemental forces of Nature.

In this respect, the celebrated wild child of Aveyron, discovered by the no less celebrated Professor Itard, appears to have shown much more varied and detailed signs of a profound and spontaneous life amid the forces of Nature, although he was observed only in captivity (a gentle captivity, admittedly) or in a relative semi-freedom in a man-made park.

Itard's text ('Victor de l'Aveyron' by Jean Itard, reproduced by Lucien Malson in his book *Les Enfants sauvages*, coll. 10/18, Paris) contains descriptions of some wonderful and highly enviable states of being for a child supposed to be 'backward' – privileged states which even many of our contemporaries, overwrought by the feverish agitation of an absurd civilisation,

99

would secretly envy: 'If a stormy wind started to blow, if the sun suddenly appeared from behind the clouds, his joy was almost convulsive . . .' A snowy morning: 'His joy bursting out in piercing cries, he runs and rolls in the snow . . .' 'He remained there for part of the night, standing motionless, his neck stretched, his eyes fixed on the countryside illuminated by the moon' . . . etc. (*Rapport*, 1801).

After several years of this uprooted urban existence: 'He still continues to show himself sensitive to the joys of his primitive life. He has the same passion for the countryside, the same ecstasy at the sight of a beautiful moonlight or a snow-covered field, the same raptures at the sound of a stormy wind' . . . 'A still unextinguished passion which a beautiful summer evening or the sight of a deeply shaded wood is enough to rekindle . . . (*Lettres à Monsieur de Talleyrand*, 1806).

Itard describes the child's joy when contemplating a flame, 'a dancing ray of light', and his pleasure as he savours slowly, drop by drop, water which at that time had not been polluted or treated with chlorine.

* * *

A silent revolution began, a decade or two ago, concerning the 'non-human thought' of the animal world and so of wild children in general.

Challenging the old academic distinctions of 'Nature' and 'Culture', those ancient concepts, encrusted like old ivy, of instinct or innateness, some enquiring young minds across the Atlantic have discovered, for example, that crows teach their little ones, by their reactions, what a cat, a goshawk or a marten is; similarly, rats teach their young to recognise poisons; monkeys transmit 'recipes' to one another – how to clean potatoes (one monkey even *invented* a method for salting them in sea-water, taught the method to its own young, to its 'old parents', its friends and the whole tribe); the mother cat shows her kitten, by her attitude, how to acknowledge a fellow-cat with the 'nose-to-nose' gesture (on the other hand, a cat reared entirely by a human being, in isolation from other cats, is ignorant of this code).

Neither does the genetic 'programme', the source of the famous 'innate instinct', support the infallibility, the 'innateness', of an act adapted to its object: a squirrel reared in isolation from its fellow-creatures will gnaw away at a nut that it has never seen before, attacking it without success; further attempts and failures follow until, by chance, the squirrel discovers the weak point of the fruit.

Certain similarities are discernible in the 'gazelle-education' of the child of the Rio de Oro: in addition to an imitative tendency conditioned by environment, a gazelle 'culture' has almost entirely replaced a human 'culture', by an imitative process of education: rather like the medical process of blood-transfusion, a child who started from a human environment was adapted to the social pattern of a herbivorous, running ungulate.

The traditional élites of the Western bourgeoisie speak of Culture with a capital C; ethnologists extend the meaning of the word to signify the existential mental acquirements of diverse human ethnic groups.

But there is every reason to extend the term to all animals.

In the case of the child of the Rio de Oro, except for the expression of the eyes and certain other characteristics, the 'cultural' substitution would have been practically total if the child had been adopted by the gazelles in the first few days of his life.

A particularly unusual case provides a curious and revealing illustration of the 'cultural' formation of a wild child by an animal. The daughter of a famous American scientist couple, the Kellogs, was deliberately raised, from birth, in the company of a chimpanzee. To the surprise of the experimenting parents, as the monkey developed more quickly than the girl, she gradually assumed the animal's habits and gestures. Only the presence of the little girl's human parents and her humanised environment eventually enabled her to overtake the monkey.

The same substitution of 'culture' or code-system occurs when two animals of different species have been raised together, the substitution being per-petuated in each generation. A male bullfinch that had been raised with a female canary learnt only the canary's song. The male bullfinch then mated with a female of his own species; the two young offspring (males) learnt their father's canary song, which they retained into adult age. In the second generation, the same substituted acquirement was repeated.

The phenomenon of a human child receiving his 'cultural' formation from animals is illustrated in reverse by the experiments of the celebrated Professor Lorenz, who assumed the role of 'father', 'nurse' and 'educator' to some goslings and ducklings; as they grew up, the animals 'knew' only the professor and hardly 'communicated' at all with their own species.

This phenomenon, which Lorenz terms 'imprinting', also throws light on the strange cases of animals of different kinds, often enemies in their natural habitats, living peacefully together from birth. For example, in the native village of Krishna – the semi-mythical Hindu Orpheus – foxes and hens, wolves and monkeys, dogs and cats, cobras and mongooses, live together in harmony by an intercommunication of codes based on acquirements of common origin. (In addition to this curious 'recreation' of a mythical mentality, there are the experiments of the Tertre-Rouge, France, and the Wolf Park in Moscow. The phenomenon can also be observed in nature: in Haute-Provence my cat, when a kitten, somehow made the acquaintance of a young magpie. The bird, nesting in a neighbouring wood, announced its presence to the cat with certain special cries, flew down and performed a sort of coded dance around the animal, which 'replied' with strange rhythmic evolutions.)

Having managed to communicate with his wild geese, Konrad Lorenz then succeeded in transmitting 'orders' to them by imitating their codes. By making the appropriate quackings and waving his arms, running or suddenly lying down on the ground, Lorenz can control a flock of wild geese, making them take to flight and then come back to the ground.

I suppose that, simply by producing an adequate imitation of one or several series of codes and signals used by the child of the Rio de Oro and his animals, I would have been able to 'manoeuvre' the whole herd at will!

These observations are confirmed by the fact that the peasants and shepherds of Sweden and Iceland have long been accustomed to 'controlling' the flight of geese, swans and eiders by the same process of imitation.

Extraordinary cases of adoption and the 'Lorenz effect' are to be observed among animals themselves. Hens without chickens of their own raise ducklings and young turkeys. A brood-hen has been known to take two orphan cats under her wing; the cats did not seem worried by her attentions and played around the old hen as if she were their mother, even licking her feathers.

A little cardinal bird placed an insect in the open mouth of a domestic goldfish which was surfacing in the hope of a few crumbs; the bird continued to do this for several weeks, no doubt because its nest had been destroyed.

Indirectly throwing light on yet another aspect of the case of my gazelle-boy, other observers have recently begun to disentangle the old and hitherto almost insurmountable problem of animal intelligence, which has been shown to exist in several equal but different forms.

Some birds like grackles and parrots articulate human phrases, and not always without understanding them, others decorate and paint with the barbula of a reed in their beaks, design beds of moss in which they plant flowers – the bird of paradise for instance (aesthetic intelligence); certain spiders continually invent new and fantastic architectures for their webs (conceptual intelligence). The amorous 'etiquette' of a mating gnat, which 'surpasses that of the most refined civilisations' (Dr. Jacques Lecomte), could be attributed to the intelligence of sensibility.

It has recently been discovered that wolves pass 'information' to one another by means of complicated codes which include not only facial signs, but also movements of the tail and ears that reveal a close similarity with the ear and tail signals of gazelles. These codes, which have not yet been properly deciphered, would seem to indicate warnings of intentions in a system based on hierarchic rank. Wild children raised by wolves must also know something of the codes.

The whole context of the questions raised above is so broad and complex, I am led to distinguish three basic categories of wild children:

1. Those brought up by animals; their 'imprinting' varies according to the age at which the child has assumed an animal existence; these children can be subdivided into herbivorous (the gazelle-boy of Mauritania) and carnivorous.

2. Wild children who have lived in total isolation and have been conditioned wholly and exclusively by natural forces (such cases are extremely rare). The faculties of observation and anticipation are 'educated' by the environment. The slightest failure of practical intelligence, interest, attention

and adaptability to the environment can result only in rapid elimination.

This category includes the famous 'Victor of Aveyron', whose senses of smell, sight and hearing had been trained to a high degree for survival even in severe winters.

3. Children who have been placed in isolation and are not 'wild' in the strict sense of the word. Owing to the extreme weakness of the 'stimuli' received, their inventive imagination is not developed. The result is almost invariably the backward child, whom only the psychiatrist is competent to observe.

Now a rather strange question: can an animal find itself in the situation of a 'wild child' in relation to its own kind? Let us first consider the gazelle. Like the Dodecahedron of Plato with its thousand multipolar faces, an oblique light can produce the most unexpected ricochets.

I know of a gazelle reared from birth (or almost from birth) in the house of a Swiss ethnologist, in total isolation from other gazelles. It wanders among books and the sand of its desert consists of carpets on which it scatters certain marks from time to time (its territory?). A drawing-room variety, in fact: 'var. salonensis' for erudite biologists!

According to information received from the adopting 'animal', in this case the professor, it seems that the gazelle 'knows' only its master; sometimes it circles round him as a 'sign of joy', emitting whisper-like murmurs, etc. Relations are complicated by the presence of a dog reared at the same time as this desert beauty; dog and gazelle have established an even more natural 'communication' with each other – sometimes the gazelle, putting both front feet on the table, will steal a piece of ham from its master and immediately transfer it to the dog's jaws.

A German review published by the Lorenz school describes the case of a woman who reared a gazelle in her apartment with a feeding-bottle (!). The animal would push its muzzle through her child's hair, pulling it with its teeth, and, like the other gazelle, would turn in a circle round its mistress. But, when restored to semi-freedom in the desert, the animal did not know how to roll itself into a ball to protect itself against the sand during a *simoon*.

Other accounts by persons who have raised gazelles are too sentimentalised and silly to be reproduced here – the danger of the genre!

The gazelle 'imprinted' with a human environment thus retains the essential characteristics and languages of its species.

On the other hand, certain of the higher animals sometimes show a considerable degree of human imprinting, direct or indirect, especially when their natural aptitudes are utilised by man: circus bears riding motor-cycles, monkeys imitating and even caricaturing human gestures, chimpanzees dressing and eating in Western fashion (!); circus people have long possessed an empirical genius for this particular kind of imprinting.

Certain birds reared by man, such as the grackle of India, excel in this respect and are even capable of producing humorous repartee in articulate language, much to the amazement of the unforewarned. (At the Rabindranah Bhose Institute in Benares, results that would seem incredible to a Westerner, whose thinking is usually linear, have been achieved in studying the influence of the human psyche on the growth of plants and their reciprocal 'behaviour' with Man, and also in studying the 'mental' element of mimesis in general and its infinite and fantastic sign-system. A Siberian institute of telepathy is embarking on research into the 'telepathic sign-system' of animals and of children with animals.)

* * *

As I write these lines, these latter aspects of communication and imprinting have been further illuminated by the experiment undertaken by a young American couple, the Gardners, who have had the idea of communicating with chimpanzees by means of a coded sign-language based on that used by deaf mutes. The experiment has produced immediate results. The Gardners' monkeys are already capable of constructing sentences of Indo-European structure with subject, verb and complement, main clause and subordinate clause; for example: 'You and I go outside to eat bananas.' According to the latest news I have received, the monkeys are attaining semantic levels corresponding to concepts of an increasingly abstract nature.

13. FINAL QUESTIONS

The precise zoological species of my wild child's gazelles, which the Nemadis called *eddami* or *edemi*, has not been established.

One particular question, revealing the obsession of the present time, has often been put to me: the question of the boy's sexual awareness. I do not recall having seen anything special in his behaviour in this respect, even when he saw his gazelles copulating at certain periods. On reaching puberty, I think that the child will imitate the very restricted rhythm (only two or three weeks in the year, at the most) of his animals, which conform to the rhythm of other mammals; he will therefore be much less tormented by the problem than the rest of us, and especially the psycho-analysts.

With regard to the term 'Nemdaï' ('Nemadis' in the plural), the custom of the Moors is to use the term for all nomads who hunt gazelles and antelopes exclusively, or almost exclusively, over the greater part of Mauritania or the western Sahara. For the specialists, the 'true' Nemadis do not extend as far as the elevated latitudes of the *Reg* of the Tiris, not even its southern fringes.

But when a hunter, and especially a true Nemdaï, is obsessed with pursuit, how far will he not go? (Moorish proverb).

As for the mental backwardness which certain persons assume to be characteristic of wild children in general, I found no sign of this in my gazelle-boy.

Certain psychiatrists refer to specific phenomena – an insensitivity to heat and cold, to pain and burning, to colds, a fixed stare, etc. But my gazelle-boy's obvious insensitivity to the extremes of temperature is the result of having become accustomed to his environment. Any little desert nomad or European gipsy child is in the habit of going about naked in all weather; as far as I can remember, I have never noticed these children being subject to colds or to other infections of the respiratory passages.

Presumably, I myself must have acquired a similar tendency, for the more

I have lived in my great open spaces – seas, deserts and jungles, amid tempests, grey-green shadows dripping with humidity, freezing nights and diabolical winds, and usually lightly clad – the less I have found myself subject to colds and other disorders. My insensitivity to burning was due to the calluses on the soles of my feet which enabled me, like the child and the nomads, to travel over scorching ground (the gazelle-boy also had callosities on the palms of his hands). Similarly, my sensitivity to pain gradually diminished: I received a number of quite serious wounds on my body which I only discovered several hours afterwards (the child seemed more sensitive to these injuries).

As for the fixed stare, the theory of the psychiatrists obviously falls flat in the case of my protégé.

Once again, how could a retarded child, even though 'aided' by animals, continue to exist in the harsh environment of a desert? Moreover, how could he be sensitive to the life of the elements?

The only habit that might possibly denote a slightly neurotic state was the child's occasional sucking of his thumb, which became more marked after the death of his gazelle 'nurse'; this habit, though described as 'regressive' by the psycho-analysts, in no way affected the general equilibrium of his existence.

The story of the ostrich-child related by the young Nemdaï has been confirmed by Professor Monod in an article entitled 'The life of Sidi Mohamed Ould Sidia with the ostriches for ten years, related by himself'. (*Notes africaines*, Institut Français d'Afrique Noire, no. 26, April 1945, Dakar. These articles came to my knowledge as a result of correspondence with Professor Théodore Monod in 1962–3.) I have every reason to believe that the child was the same. This confirms the old popular saying that there is no smoke without fire.

My learned correspondent also drew my attention to a case similar to my own, a child who lived around the beginning of the century with a herd of Dorcas gazelles in the western Sahara (another gazelle-boy), and whose story was told by Sidi Dah Ould Haïba (op. cit.). There is also the case of a third child who lived with a lion (!) in this same part of the desert (op. cit.).

A rather odd question has often been put to me: how can wild children in general, and therefore my gazelle-boy, survive the age of puberty (the sexual problem and others)? I must admit to being somewhat baffled by the question. For me, facts have always spoken louder than theories or rules. My gazelle-boy of Spanish Mauritania is now well beyond the age of 15 (the most recent American 'intervention' would not have been organised without good reason!); the gazelle-boy of Syria was still living at liberty at the apparent age of 20–22. The wolf-child of Kronstadt was captured at the age of 23 (1885); the sow-girl of Salzburg at 22 (1831); the celebrated Kaspar Hauser of Nuremberg at 18 (1832); the bear-girl of Karpfen (Hungary) at 18 (1767); Jean of Liége at 21 (1744); the girl of Kranenburg (Holland) at 19 (Linnaeus, 1717), etc. (Lucien Malson, op. cit.: Bibliography, p. 125.)

In the course of the hullabaloo that broke out in the newspapers just as this book was about to go to press, I had the good fortune to discover some photographs, allegedly of the gazelle-boy of Syria and taken at the time of his capture in 1946. On one photograph the child, bound hand and foot, is seen scowling; no gazelle appears on the photograph. A second photograph shows him seated, his legs to one side, holding in both hands a tuft of thorn-bush and making as if to eat it; this second photograph, which has little of the authentic wild child about it, appears to have been 'staged' for reasons unknown (Photo: Hamid, Cairo).

The first photograph does show a resemblance to my gazelle-boy, especially in the case of the ankles (though on the photograph the child's ankles are less thick), thus justifying the theory of physical similarities deriving from similarities of function. The weaknesses of the second photograph, on the other hand, cause one to doubt whether this is in fact the gazelle-boy of Syria (though the child certainly existed).

* * *

As I approach the end of my book, I am beginning to realise that I have found myself, unwittingly, on the edge of a volcano of myths and symbols that have nurtured the dreams, hopes and beliefs of men since their first animal origins.

The function of the shaman, the first 'avatar' of those myths and symbols, has been defined thus by the scholarly mythologist Mircea Eliade: in attempting through mysticism and ecstasy to liberate himself from man's present 'degraded' condition, the shaman seeks to rediscover a primordial purity – the 'beyond' (or the 'hither') of the ancient interdiction represented by the symbolic fall, a characteristic of all religions.

A shamanist séance comprises the following stages: the summoning of the 'auxiliary spirits', often animals, and a 'dialogue' with them in a secret language; the playing of drums and dancing to prepare the mystical journey 'in time'; and finally, the trance of 'disconnection'. The shaman utters cries and grunts in lifelike imitation of the sounds of birds and mammals, assuming all the attitudes of the animal that is 'relived' (tiger-men, panther-men, wolf-men, etc.); the 'retrocession' is thus a return to origins, to 'Homo Primigenius', Primitive or Primordial Man, the archetype of the Adam-Kadmon of Totality finally rediscovered and regained: the universal animism of humanity's participation in its own dawn.

This state of transposition and transparence, of primary reintegration, is often induced with the aid of drugs for the 'journey': the mistletoe of the Druids, the *amanita muscaria* and black nightshade of the shaman-healers, the Aztec mushroom called the 'Flesh-of-the-Gods' etc. – all 'levers' of unsuspected importance whose full implications the present age of repression is not yet capable of grasping.

* * *

Even before I have completed my manuscript, the gazelle-boy of the Sahara has prompted a totally unforeseeable ground-swell.

Quite apart from all the superficial discussion and the anecdotes, I sense an immense, unconscious and unformulated need to rediscover an obscure, primeval Elsewhere, some archetypal *noumenon* of primordial reintegration within and around oneself – above all because of our experience of this fragmented, atomised, polluted, directionless life offering only the sombre and deadly prospect of an increasingly anonymous technocracy.

Already, it seems, wild children living and communicating with animals have become the reincarnation of the old universal myths, the myths of

Orpheus and Krishna and others. The proof lies in the fact that imagination, feminine and intuitive, has not yet been reduced to silence and nothingness by the Promethean Father with the frozen stare of a giant computer, and, even more strikingly, in the mighty movement of gestation in which more and more young people all over the world are returning to 'primordial participation' in the new era that is dawning and which some call 'Aquarius' – when 'intercommunicability' will gradually extend to all minds, despite the restrictions and dogmas of the stubbornly enduring past: the image of a new Shamanic participation, from the very first animate beings to interplanetary exchanges; if not this, then a crazy self-centredness with the visage of thermonuclear chaos.

* * *

And so I have reached the end of my strange adventure with a primitive child living in the light of his sands and his wind-footed animals, observed by an obscure witness whose own life was in turmoil at the time and who, thanks to a 'gazelle-boy' in his lost desert, was able to rediscover the freshness and lightness of a morning unknown to the human heart . . . and, at the same time, to set the skulls of philosophers in a ferment.

O my improbable child of the sands, sung to the accompaniment of the twelve-stringed lute by the high-pitched voices of the Moorish women with their long night-blue veils, under the nomad tents! (They are my best witnesses, these poor people of the 'Third World' whom no one in the West has yet thought of questioning. . . . The testimony of the poor carries no weight.)

POSTSCRIPT

POSTSCRIPT

In the course of the curious storm that began even before this book appeared, I received telephone calls and letters from numerous countries in Europe and even from more distant parts, inviting me to undertake research on artificially-induced 'wild children': for example, on a human baby that was to be taken from its mother and put in a nature reserve to be raised by a wolf of the Siberian steppes – the experiment would be applied, in reverse and simultaneously, to the wolf's cub, which was to be taken from its own mother! A professor in the U.S.A. has offered me free facilities for research in a specially created environment with technical aids. But neither money nor outrageous proposals which, however logical from the scientific point of view, revolt my conscience, will persuade me to deviate from my own little interior light.

At the same time, I respect the courageous youth of two currents of civilisation whose eyes are undoubtedly turned to the future.

To satisfy everyone, without losing my soul and my freedom of action, I make this suggestion: I shall be ready to travel to any part of the world and to any climate where reliable information points to the existence of other wild children, but on this one condition – that any such children, as soon as they are discovered, are left unmolested in their natural habitat and in the environment of their adoptive animals.

APPENDIX

APPENDIX

I must here add, by way of comparison, the account (*Notes africaines*, no. 26, April 1945) given by Sidi Dah Ould Haïba, of Dakar, of the gazelle-boy of the Aftout-es-Saheli (former French Mauritania):

Among the Moors, as soon as a child is born, if its mother's milk is insufficient and if there is no woman in the encampment who can feed it with her own milk, a sheep, a goat or even a cow is chosen to suckle it at the desired times.

Listen to this curious happening which only Allah is capable of devising!

In one of the numerous nomad encampments in the Aftout, a woman gave birth to a little boy. Unable to feed it with her own milk, she chose an animal for the purpose, as is the custom; but, instead of a goat or a sheep, she chose a beautiful gazelle which she had had for several years and which she loved dearly. Each time the gazelle gave its abundant milk to its mistress's little one. The gazelle was gentle, very gentle. Instinctively, it knew when the child wanted to suck; always, at the proper time, it would arrive in front of the tent bleating. It never moved far from the camp.

When the child had grown and could crawl on all fours, then walk a little, he would go up to the gazelle whenever he saw it in the vicinity; when the gazelle saw him, it would start to bleat, part its legs, place itself in the appropriate position and allow the child to suck its milk. The gazelle had a rope round its neck with which it was tethered near the child in the evening. The child, familiar with his nurse, always enjoyed himself with her. He was always seen holding the end of the rope, going everywhere the gazelle led him.

One day, in the mother's absence, the child took the end of his nurse's rope, as usual, and began to play with her. The gazelle led him out of the encampment to graze and then, when it saw a herd of gazelles, its wild instincts were reawakened and it wanted to join them – the child, unwittingly, still holding the end of the rope.

The wild herd watched their comrade approaching; some males, wanting to go up to her, saw the human child, stopped abruptly and then, realising the truth, turned round and disappeared into a thicket. This was the signal for the whole herd, which followed them at full speed.

The gazelle still followed them, browsing as it went and stopping each time the child wanted to suck. It continued for several days, wandering further and further into the arid desert, still following the herd's traces.

At midday, it allowed the child to sleep under a tree and remained by his side until he woke up; at night, it did the same. Numerous gazelles would approach them, flee, and then come back. Eventually, they realised that the little one was harmless for the simple reason that one of their comrades was beside him without being in danger. They familiarised themselves with the couple, as did all the gazelles in the region.

Thereafter, he lived among these wild animals, who gave him all their attention. Since he was past the suckling age and his nurse had no more milk, he now ate only the leaves of trees, grass, etc. He lived as an herbivorous animal. He was agile and supple, but, on the other hand, he was timid: the slightest rustle or noise would make him run for several hours. He went with the herd as it moved from one region to another in search of copious pastures and followed its migrations. When it was time to sleep, at night or for the siesta, he always lay beside his nurse, who would awaken him at the appropriate time with caresses, licking his face and hands. As his protectress, she would always warn him first in the event of danger: running as well as the gazelles, he was always in the middle of the fleeing band. If another gazelle pushed him aside, kicked him or butted him with its horns, it would have to answer to the child's nurse, which would immediately charge at it and drive it away with its horns or by kicking out at it and perhaps even breaking one of its limbs.

Several years passed thus. He had grown tall and was observed by hunters on several occasions, but he always managed to escape, thanks to his great speed.

One day he found himself surrounded by several men and captured, his nurse having fled with the others. He was taken to an encampment, but it was a long time before he could speak and accustom himself to the diet; eventually, however, he could manage everything. Sometimes, when engaged in a serious conversation in a group, he would suddenly rush at a plant which he thought sweet or a piece of grass, swallowing it greedily and then resuming his place in the group.

He had not seen his nurse since the day when they had been separated. One day, as he was hunting, he saw several gazelles grazing in a fine meadow. [To a Moor, a few dozen tufts of hard grass per hectare can seem a 'fine meadow'.] He lay in wait for them: none of the gazelles had noticed him. He wondered how he was going to get a shot at one of them; he was quite far away and none of them had detached itself from the group. He had just decided to fire at the whole herd when a beautiful female detached herself from the rest and took a few paces towards him. He fired. Bang! She fell motionless. Happy at his success, he took his dagger and strode towards the animal to slit its throat. As he stooped over it, the knife in his right hand and his left hand pressing against the victim's throat, he recognised his nurse.

He dropped dead of grief and regret, his hands squeezing her tightly. ('The Story of Eddami, the gazelle'. *Eddami* = korin gazelle. The Aftout is a region of Mauritania situated in the Sahel zone, far from the Tiris. The Moors and Nemadis do not confuse this story with that of the gazelle-boy of the Tiris, neither do the two cases correspond in time.)

* * *

There is also the recent and highly intriguing case of a wild child discovered in France (Loire-Atlantique) in 1962; in fact, this child was only semi-wild, because he was subsequently 're-educated' and had not even lost his original name (little Yves Cheneau). I will end by quoting in full the story of the ostrich-child Sidi Mohamed who lived 'with the ostriches for ten years' – an account unique in that it comes from his own mouth. (This is probably the same child as in the story related by my young Nemdaï.) Sidi Mohamed is another case of a 'semi-wild' child, since he too was 're-educated' and had retained his original name (cases of semi-wild children must be much more numerous, though this aspect of the subject has not yet been fully elucidated – the wild life is adopted at a relatively late stage and the child nearly always returns to the world of men at the age of puberty):

It seems that when she was suckling me my mother used to say that I would have to be watched or I would get lost one day; at the age of about five or six years, I used to go out with other children and play outside the tents, and then one day I disappeared for no reason. I was in the bush for three days without anything.

But Allah the Great wanted to save me. One fine morning, I was walking quietly along thinking of nothing – I was very young and couldn't care less. Suddenly, I saw something gleaming in the sunlight: ostrich eggs, some already hatched, the others not. I was a little surprised, but I stayed there for a while; then I saw a pair of ostriches appear, the male and the female. Naturally, they were surprised to see me beside their eggs. Eventually, they got used to me, after three days together. I was now part of the family!

My life with my foster-parents, as it were.

This is how we spent the time: very early in the morning the male would get up and flap his wings, waking all of us; I would get up, and the female too. Finally, we were on our way amid nature. After travelling a good distance, we passed the siesta under the bushy trees. I would lie down or sit, as I chose.

My temporary parents ate bones, stones, leaves from trees and everything edible in this bush country. I ate green grass. In the evening we would return from our grazing, happy as a herd returning to the zeriba [Enclosure for the night].

When grazing, I always stayed with these beautiful animals. If sometimes I felt weary, which happened very rarely, my friends would slow down and wait for me. I was extraordinarily healthy, I was hairy, I did not know the meaning of the word fever, I could run as well as my ostrich-parents, and I felt that these animals with their silky plumes were very happy throughout my stay with them.

At night, when we returned from grazing, these were our positions: I lay with the chicks, the mother to our right, the father to our left, both covering us with their wings, which protected us from the cold. There were two families of ostriches and I was on good terms with both, but I was more cherished by the family with which I was living.

This is what we did during the season of hibernation [the hot and rainy season when life slows down – midsummer; in Europe the word is used in the opposite sense, i.e. the winter]. When it rained and we were out of the nest, we huddled together under a tree; when it rained on us in the nest, the chicks and I stayed under the parents' wings until the last drops. During hibernation we would drink from ponds or eat green grass; sometimes we were without water for six or seven days.

In the dry season this is what happened: my parents did not care about water; when I was grazing I would come across a few water-melons which I always found refreshing, whether they were sweet or bitter, and also the green leaves of the trees. This is how I lived during the dry season.

My cruel separation from the ostriches.

One fine day, as we were quietly grazing, about one o'clock in the afternoon, I saw three armed horsemen appear: they were ostrich-hunters. As soon as they saw us, they began to chase us, from one o'clock until nightfall. I was with the ostriches, running as well as they. It was growing dark, my parents had vanished into nature, and the horsemen finally caught me. They had to make some ropes with *titaricks* [a local rope], with which they fastened me astride one of the horses, behind the saddle, my hands and feet under the horse's belly, and they took me to the camp. Throughout the journey I kept butting my enemy with my head. As soon as we arrived at the tents, I was fastened with an iron chain under a tree, where I spent about one week. I was then freed and I stayed for two or three months; then my real parents came to fetch me.

It took me a long time to get used to the customs of the country and the climate, which I found irksome. I did not like the food and ate very little; sometimes I would go out into the bush to eat a little grass.

I was also pestered for information about the ostriches. I was almost a deaf mute and did not reply to the endless questions put to me; however, gradually I became accustomed to living like human beings and I emerged from my savage state.

This is how I spent some ten years with these beautiful animals whose memory I shall always cherish, and I hate the types who hunt them. ('The life of Sidi Mohamed with the ostriches for ten years. The scene of these events was the Assaba, the dangerous, according to me Beyboune.' – The text was drawn up by Sidi Beyboune from the mouth of Sidi Mohamed Ould Sidia Ould Mohamed, Taguat division, Circle of Kaédi, and included in a collection of documents prepared by M. Cournarie, former Governor-General of French Mauritania. *Notes africaines*, no. 26, April 1945.)

The two cases quoted above demonstrate the astounding fact that two children living with animals which, though of utterly different zoological types, were both capable of running at great speed, were enabled by 'imprinting' to run as fast as their 'parents' – all the more reason why my young gazelle-boy of the central Rio de Oro, whose whole life has been lived in such conditions, should not have proved an exception to this law.

BIBLIOGRAPHY

BIBLIOGRAPHY

I. On the gazelle-boy of the Spanish Sahara (Western Sahara): *The author usually quoted under his private name : Jean-Claude Auger.*

Informations UNESCO, October 1963.

Match 'Télématch', 12 October 1963, no. 757, Paris.

Science et Nature, Communiqué, no. 58, November 1963, Paris (Muséum).

Notes africaines, I.F.A.N., April 1963, pp. 58–61 (article by Prof. Théodore Monod, Director of the Institut Français d'Afrique Noire, member of the Institut de France: 'Un enfant-gazelle au Sahara Occidental').

In ATTILIO GAUDIO, *Les Civilisations du Sahara*, pp. 230–2 (coll. Livres de poche 'Marabout-Université'), Paris.

In LUCIEN MALSON, *Les Enfants sauvages* (coll. 10/18), Paris (pp. 52, 75 and 114 in the 1969 edition).

Revista de Estudios Scientíficas y Humanidades, Buenos-Aires Universidad, October 1965, pp. 1225–7 (vol. XXXII).

Artzen dena Igurra, University of San Sebastian (in exile at Santiago in Chile), pp. 884–7 (vol. XIII), 1966, text in Basque (Euzkadi-Sud).

DR. SAYAWASA, *Animal teaching: gazelle in West Africa, other animals and little wolf of India.* Advanced Science Institute, Rabindranah Bhose University, Benares, October 1968.

Nara University, *Structures and evolution of spirit about a wild child taught by gazelles in West African desert* (Dr. Mitsuko Marabushi), February 1969. Tokyo, 1221, 1 Chome 6, Shikoku Press, Japan.

Lectures on the child of the Rio de Oro : at the Fondation Teilhard de Chardin (November 1969, Muséum, Paris); at the Institut d'Anthropologie, Geneva (Prof. Sauter, December 1970); at the Institut d'Ethnographie (Prof. Gabus) and at the University of Neuchâtel (Switzerland, January 1971); at the Institut de la Vie, Muséum (Dr. Rouget), Geneva, etc.

Numerous press articles in Switzerland, France and other countries. Radio and TV in Switzerland and France (pre-publication), February 1971.

II. On wild children in general:

J.-J. ROUSSEAU, *Discours sur l'origine de l'inégalité parmi les hommes*, Geneva 1754. And on the two bear-children of the Pyrenees: Presentation to King Louis XV of the 'two savages' by the Intendant of Gascony, Archives Préfectorales of the city of Toulouse.

CH.-M. DE LA CONDAMINE, *Histoire d'une jeune fille sauvage trouvée dans les bois à l'âge de 10 ans*, Paris 1755. Presentation to the King by the Intendant of Champagne and the Bishop of Langres.

J.-M. G. ITARD, *De l'Education du jeune sauvage de l'Aveyron*, Paris 1801. Report made to Monsieur de Talleyrand, 1807. Imprimerie impériale.

On Kaspar Hauser, numerous articles and books. But this child, whose case is too often quoted, had probably been subjected to total isolation and was not a 'wild child' in the strict sense of the term.

MARIA MONTESSORI, *Pédagogie scientifique. Itard et le sauvage de l'Aveyron*, 1926.

W. N. KELLOG, P. C. SQUIRES, *New York Times*, etc.: numerous publications between 1926 and 1934 on the Reverend Singh's two wolf-girls of India, Kamala and Amala.

J. A. L. SINGH, *Wolf children and feral man*, New York, Harper, 1942. The great work on Amala and Kamala, written in collaboration with Professor Zingg of the University of Denver, Colorado.

CLAUDE LEVI-STRAUSS, *Les Structures élémentaires de la parenté* (Chap. I, 'Nature et Culture'), Presses Universitaires de France, Paris 1949. The Jansenist approach of the great ethnologist, who regards the majority of wild children as mentally-retarded rejects, is far too systematic and facile. Specific cases only.

ANDRE DEMAISON, *Le Livre des enfants sauvages*, Paris, ed. André Bonne, 1953 (1st edn.).

MAURICE MERLEAU-PONTY, *Les Relations avec autrui chez l'enfant*, Collège de France, C.D.U., 1958, Paris. The celebrated and fashionable philosopher of 'Tout-Paris' regards mutism in *homo ferus* as the consequence of an affective frustration and a privation of social contacts. Such a system of thought is still too abstract and too rigorous. In the case of children adopted by animals at a very early age, what affection would there be to frustrate? And are 'social contacts' characteristic only of the human order?

LUCIEN MALSON, Professor of Social Psychology at the Centre National de Pédagogie at Beaumont-Oise (France): *Les Enfants sauvages*, followed by *Mémoire et rapport sur Victor de l'Aveyron* by JEAN ITARD (collection 10/18, Union générale d'Editions, Paris); numerous new editions since 1964.

DR. SEU TCHOU LI, *Kamala, Amala and wild children in Old China*, Hong Kong, 1968. The author seems to be unaware of the codes used by wolves among themselves, a discovery made by some Canadian authors in 1966. One of the Reverend Singh's two wolf-girls, who survived for quite a long time, would have been able to learn much more in the articulation of human words if her second educator had used the coded signal-system of the wolves as a transitional 'language' (but such a 'language' was obviously unknown at the time).

In the case of my gazelle-boy, it was already too late to use a transitional grammatical code of this kind. And, in any case, it was not my intention to allow this child to become part of the technological cretinism of our present civilisation (a gazelle-boy dressed up in business-suit and tie!). Even worse than in the time of the Reverend Singh!